An Official Tribute and History of
THE ROYAL OBSERVER CORPS

Henry Buckton

ASHFORD, BUCHAN & ENRIGHT
LEATHERHEAD

First published in 1993 by
Ashford, Buchan & Enright, Publishers,
31 Bridge Street, Leatherhead, Surrey KT22 8BN

British Library Cataloguing in Publication Data

ISBN 1 85253 292 0

Photograph acknowledgements
Where permission has been granted for the reproduction
of photographs, the source has been quoted within the caption,
with the exception of the following: photograph of Air Commodore
Donaldson, with the permission of HQ No 11 Group RAF;
photograph of the Prime Minister, with the permission of the Press Office,
10 Downing Street; and photograph of Air Chief Marshal Sir Michael
Graydon, with the permission of HQ UK Air Forces/HQ
Strike Command. Back cover with the permission of Mara McGregor.
The abbreviation ROCM in captions, refers to the
Royal Observer Corps Museum, Winchester.

Contents

Acknowledgements

First, I would like to thank Michael Marks (Hon. Sec. of ROCA), Joyce Shrubbs (Chairman of ROCA) and John Murphy (Chairman of the ROC Benevolent Fund), for reading and approving the manuscript, and making relevant amendments. Thanks to Alan Price-Talbot (ex-Southern Area Commandant), for not only doing most of the research into the history of early warning systems, but helping to fill in some vital gaps as well. Thanks also to Obs Lt Neville Cullingford, curator of the ROC Museum, Winchester, for providing most of the photographs. Ronald Mathews, Public Relations Officer at Tangmere, himself an ex-chief observer, also deserves thanks. Thanks to Michael Virtue of Virtue and Co Ltd Publishers, Haltwhistle, for quotes from *Hutchinson's Pictorial History of the War*. Thanks to Miriam Sharland of Colour Library Books for quotes from Roy Conyers Nesbit's *An Illustrated History of the RAF* and Ivor Matanle's *World War II*. Thanks to Richard Riding, Editor of *Aeroplane Monthly*, for quotes from A.C. Trinder's article 'Forewarmed is Forearmed'. Thanks to Wg-Cdr Roy Davies, composer of 'Skywatch', for useful information, and to Wg-Cdr H.B. Hingley, RAF Music and Jane Pettit, Boosey and Hawkes Music Publishers Ltd, for the extract. Thanks to Obs Lt P.J. Proost at HQ ROC for quotes from the *ROC Journal*. Thanks to Stephen Woolford, Duxford Museum; Air Vice-Marshal F.C. Hurrell from the RAF Benevolent Fund; Wg-Cdr N. Hancock, Hon. Sec. of the Battle of Britain Fighter Association; and John Dawkins, Publicity Wing RAF Inspectorate of Recruiting, for useful addresses. Thanks go to Air Commodore Donaldson for providing the Foreword to the book, and to Sir Kenneth Scott, Private Secretary to the Queen, for preparing for publication the Queen's address to the Corps. And of course, very special thanks to Her Majesty, who, on 11 May 1992, graciously granted the ROC Association her Royal Patronage, for allowing the address to be published.

Foreword

The close association between the Royal Observer Corps and the Royal Air Force goes back over 63 years to 1 January 1929, when the responsibility for the Corps was transferred from the War Office to the Air Ministry and the first Commandant was appointed.

The relationship between the Royal Observer Corps and the Royal Air Force was forged during the Second World War, and in recognition of the Corps' distinguished service during the Battle of Britain King George the Sixth granted the title Royal in 1941. The men and women of the Corps provided vital support throughout the war not only to Fighter Command, but also to other Home Commands. On cessation of hostilities the Corps was stood down for 6 months and then reformed to continue its voluntary work in aircraft identification and reporting until 1955 when it embraced the challenge of the nuclear reporting role. A task it carried out with efficiency and distinction for the next 36 years.

The momentous changes in eastern Europe over the past 12 months have been most welcome, but with them has come the end of the Corps' role as the field force of the United Kingdom Warning and Monitoring Organisation. On 30 September 1991 the Corps was stood down for the second time in its history with the exception of a small element which continues to serve the Royal Air Force at Nuclear Reporting Cells.

The loyalty and selfless dedication shown by the volunteer members of the Royal Observer Corps over the past 63 years is unique in our island's history and yet, with typical modesty, the volunteers do not consider their services to be in any way exceptional - they are of course wrong.

Air Commodore Michael Donaldson, MBE, RAF
Commandant Royal Observer Corps
Senior Air Staff Officer No 11 Group RAF

10 DOWNING STREET

THE PRIME MINISTER

As someone who was born during the Second
World War and who lived through the whole of
the Cold War period I am delighted to have the
opportunity of paying tribute to the work of
the Royal Observer Corps with its dedicated
band of volunteers.

The Corps did magnificent service throughout
the war and then showed its adaptability by
becoming the field force for the United
Kingdom Warning and Monitoring Organisation
where it played a vital role in our civil
defence arrangements.

We in the United Kingdom are fortunate in
being able to rely on voluntary effort in many
fields. The Corps had been an outstanding
example of how large numbers of volunteers are
prepared to give freely of their time and
effort for the good of their fellow-
countrymen. It is a record of service of which
all members of the Corps can be justly proud.

John Major

Air Chief Marshal Sir Michael Graydon KCB CBE RAF

Air Officer Commanding-in-Chief Strike Command

The Royal Observer Corps' connection with the Royal Air Force, in earlier days with Fighter Command and later with Strike Command, is a close and valued relationship. It encompasses not only the period prior to and during World War II, but also subsequently when the Corps, whilst retaining its unrivalled aircraft recognition skills, provided a nuclear warning and monitoring service to us, as well as to the Home Office. This service has been freely given by a dedicated and remarkable collection of men and women and has served the nation wonderfully well.

Although that part of the Corps which formed the field force of the United Kingdom Warning and Monitoring Organisation has been stood down as a result of the demise of the Cold War, an element still serves the Royal Air Force. I trust that our association, not to mention our affection for each others' Services, will continue long into the future not least because to be forewarned is to be forearmed.

I offer my admiration and gratitude to the Corps for its decades of selfless service.

Michael Graydon

Address by Her Majesty Queen Elizabeth II, Air Commodore-in-Chief, Royal Observer Corps

BUCKINGHAM PALACE

Fifty years ago, my father granted you the title ''Royal Observer Corps'' in recognition of your contribution to victory in the Battle of Britain. It so happens that it is also fifty years since women joined the Corps. The master-mind of the Battle of Britain was Lord Dowding, and it is fitting that this anniversary should be celebrated here at Bentley Priory, which was both his and the Corps' headquarters in those critical days.

That battle was only the beginning of the Corps' invaluable services during the last War. Apart from the routine reporting of enemy aircraft, the Corps played a most important part in the rescue of many Fighter and Bomber crews and was instrumental in the saving of the lives of many aircrew.

Later on, the Corps had an active part in our defences against the Flying Bomb campaign and it also provided a large force of Seaborne Observers in support of the Normandy landings.

The demand for your services did not end
with the War. In addition to supporting the
Royal Air Force, the Corps was given the task
of reporting nuclear incidents to the Home
Office. That was during what became known as
the Cold War. That War has now also,
thankfully, come to an end and there has been
a welcome reduction in international tensions.

While no one can predict what the future
holds, the immediate threats which gave the
Corps the reason for its existence have
receded. This means an honourable Stand Down
for the Corps after sixty-six years of
dedicated service.

When I presented the first Banner in 1966, I
said I was proud and happy to be opening a
new chapter in the history of the Corps. In
presenting you with this new Banner I am
aware that there will now be mixed feelings,
but foremost you must feel a deep sense of
pride in the knowledge that all members have
done their duty with selfless devotion.

It will be many years before the ''old
comrades'' can no longer pass on the stories
and traditions of the Corps, and even then
the record will remain and this Banner will
continue to represent the volunteer spirit
which has been such a fundamental part of the
philosophy of the Corps ever since it was
founded.

This Banner salutes sixty-six years of
dedicated voluntary service and it will
ensure that that service will never be
forgotten. I have had the honour to be your

Air Commodore-in-Chief for the last thirty-eight years, and I want to thank each one of you most warmly for all the time and effort you have given to the Royal Observer Corps. I offer you all my very best wishes for the future.

25th July, 1991

The above address, which was given by Her Majesty the Queen during the Royal Review at Bentley Priory on 25 July 1991, was graciously provided for publication by Sir Kenneth Scott, Private Secretary to Her Majesty.

Air Chief Marshal Sir Christopher Foxley-Norris
Chairman: The Battle of Britain Fighter Association

The Royal Observer Corps was inaugurated with the specific function of identifying and giving warning of enemy air attack on the United Kingdom. To some extent it was therefore suspended by Radio Direction Finding (later RADAR). A chain of various types of RDF stations was gradually established and took over these main functions. But the Royal Observer Corps was by no means totally replaced. The main RDF stations were visible and vulnerable to air attack and to jamming (although little of the latter was attempted in the early stages of the war); it could also be swamped by sheer weight of numbers. The observation posts and collecting centres of the Observer Corps continued to provide essential back-up and cross-cover even when RADAR was fully developed. In the post-war period the identification of nuclear fall-out was added to its responsibilities.

The Observer Corps also served a secondary purpose. During World War II there were a large number of competent people very keen to perform some service to the war effort, people who for various reasons, age, gender, physical limitations etc., could not take a full part in the fighting services. Such volunteers have for a long time played a most valuable part in ensuring our success in war. The ROC was one of the last and largest of such voluntary bodies. It gave to a number of our best people a genuine feeling of participation and contribution to an essential war-service. The loss of such a truly volunteer body will be a loss to our society as a whole.

Introduction

On 30 September 1991, the Royal Observer Corps was 'stood down'. The corps could boast a proud history that had begun in 1925, and during the Second World War it had formed an integral part of the United Kingdom's early warning system. Since the 1950s, it had been employed as the field force of the United Kingdom Warning and Monitoring Organisation (UKWMO), responsible for the collection, movement, and processing of information concerning nuclear bursts and the resulting radioactive fallout, following a nuclear strike on this country.

From earliest times, when people first gathered together to form settlements and villages, there had been a need for early warning systems, to warn against the approach of strangers, an attack by another tribe, or even the presence of dangerous animals. The earliest warning systems would have used every conceivable method – the simple cry of a human voice, the banging of a stone against a rock, blowing through a cattle horn, all provided effective signals.

As civilizations became established and communications improved, these early warning systems became more and more sophisticated. The Old Testament refers several times to beacons, for instance (Isaiah 30:17): 'One thousand shall flee at the rebuke of one; at the rebuke of five shall ye flee: till ye be left as a beacon upon the top of a mountain, and as an ensign on an hill.' And Jeremiah (6:1) describes a slightly more advanced system: 'O ye children of Benjamin, gather yourselves to flee out of the midst of Jerusalem, and blow the trumpet in Tekoa, and set up a sign of fire in Beth-haccerem: for evil appeareth out of the north, and great destruction.'

Agamemnon, one of the plays of the *Oresteia* trilogy by Aeschylus, first performed in 458 BC, is full of references to beacons and early warning systems. Set at the time of the siege of Troy, one character, a watchman (a sort of prototype

1

observer), remarks: 'But I'm no star-gazer. Clytemnestra stationed me here to wake her when the beacon shall flame in the east proclaiming Troy has fallen ... I must say my futile, nightly prayer: "Zeus, end my watch, light up the beacon, destroy Troy." ' Ironically, Aeschylus died as a result of a sort of aerial attack. An eagle, mistaking his bald head for a stone, dropped a tortoise in order to crack its shell. It struck Aeschylus, killing him as he sat talking with friends.

The Incas of Peru had a network of communication posts between the capital of their empire, Cuzco, and their provincial cities. Inca rulers knew almost at once about anything that was happening within the empire. *Chasquis* – express couriers, effectively – used a relay system to deliver messages speedily, waiting in roadside posts and, when a message arrived, running on with it to the next post, where the *chasqui* there would take over. In this way news from the most remote corner of the empire could reach the Sapa Inca at Cuzco in a matter of days.

The islands that collectively make up the United Kingdom have been no strangers to attack and invasion, and through the centuries a variety of early warning systems have been used to protect them. In Saxon times there were numerous beacons around the country, great stacks of wood placed ready to be lit to warn of Viking incursions or other dangers. Later, the Plantagenet King Edward III, who reigned from 1327 to 1377, ordered that beacons in Kent should be pitch-pots mounted on poles.

Perhaps the most celebrated beacons were those used in the reign of Queen Elizabeth I (1558-1603). In 1588, the Spanish King Philip II sent the Armada to attack England. To warn of this, beacons were set alight all around the countryside. An extract from *The Perambulations of Kent* by William Lambarde, published in 1570, reads:

> In war swiftness is valued no less than force itself. So the Right Honourable Sir William Brooke, the Lord Chamberlain of Queen Elizabeth's household and Lieutenant of Kent, foreseeing how necessary it was to have the forces of the country speedily drawn together to encounter an enemy,

discovered that upon the lighting of a beacon which is erected for that purpose, all types of common men and even those of place and honour did not know where to rally. Therefore through ignorance, as likely to run away from the affected area, as to run to its aid, Sir William decided to plot the locations of the beacons on a card with directional lines and routes clearly shown, by which any man with little effort may discover where lies the danger and thereafter warn his neighbours.

For example, suppose our first beacon standing upon Shooters Hill be lit. He that will go there will be advised by the watchmen from whence they received their signal, which must either be from London Town or Hampstead in the west, or Stone near Deptford in the east.

Now if any man shall think that revealing the positions of the beacons is not a fit point to be made public; I ask him to give me leave to differ. For as the value to the Realm and its subjects is obvious, in that it speeds service, where speed is essential; also there is no secret hereby disclosed. Seeing that all beacons stand open for all to see and all men know what they are for, though few men know the best use and advantages of them. Furthermore the enemy is deterred when he sees that we can and do make so good and ready use of our beacons. If however your argument is that the common people shall not be permitted to run to the affected place, as was the practice and that only the trained soldiery shall go to the appointed place - I would answer that whatsoever course be taken the quick and widespread warning of danger is of greater value for without it we are vulnerable. Also it follows that without speedy warning there will be no use for the beacons at all and they may just as well be torn down thus saving the country continual and great expense of maintaining them. As no doubt the necessity of beacons is apparent, would it not be better to spread the alarm even faster by equipping each beacon with some horsemen, anciently called Hobeliers from the hobbies [small horses or ponies] or nags, who may stay by the fire, which on a bright shining day is anyway not so well seen, so that the

Hobeliers might gallop from beacon to beacon to ensure the alarm is well and quickly spread.

It is interesting to note that when the book was republished in 1596, it contained a map of the 'Beacons in Kent'. As a result Lambarde was severely criticized for revealing state secrets, although the controversy in fact helped to restore the beacon system which had served the country so well in 1588. It is most fitting, therefore, that the badge of the Royal Observer Corps depicts one of these beacon-lighters from the time of the first Queen Elizabeth.

In the late eighteenth and early nineteenth centuries, the United Kingdom again found itself under threat from foreign invasion, this time from the French armies of Napoleon Bonaparte. A network of telegraph stations was established in threatened areas of the country, which could communicate with each other by means of a mechanical semaphore. Using this system it was possible to send a message from Plymouth to the Admiralty in London in as little as ten minutes. Local militias were recruited around the south of England, to provide a force that was ready to defend the homeland. The invasion was never to take place, however, simply because the French could not achieve superiority at sea. Their fleet, and with it all hope of invasion, was shattered at Trafalgar in 1805.

England's next real threat was to come from a completely new direction, air attack! During the First World War, Germany employed both airships and aeroplanes to bring death and destruction to the United Kingdom. The early warning system which evolved due to these attacks ultimately led to the formation of the Observer Corps. The idea of forming an Observer Corps existed in embryo towards the end of the First World War, and the first groups were raised in 1925. Through the years since the end of the Second World War the function of the Corps kept apace with modern times, and although Britain enjoyed a long period of little conflict, the Royal Observer Corps evolved to perform a series of practical roles against any future aggression, or within the continuing peace of the nation itself.

The following narrative traces the ROC's history, and the

events which moulded it. The two definitive corps histories, *Forewarned is Forearmed* by T. E. Winslow and *Attack Warning Red* by Derek Wood, give far more comprehensive accounts, but I hope that what is presented here will be understood and enjoyed by those with little or no previous knowledge of the subject. Primarily, it is a tribute to the men and women who served the corps between 1925 and 1991. I hope the book captures a little of the unique spirit of the Royal Observer Corps, and reflects the warmth and affection which so many people had for the organization throughout the kingdom.

HENRY BUCKTON
April 1993

CHAPTER ONE
Formation of the Observer Corps

The first two Observer Corps groups were formed in 1925 at
Maidstone in Kent and Horsham in Sussex. In writing a history
of any subject, it is easy enough to state facts and figures and
quote dates, but where the Royal Observer Corps is concerned
it is essential to understand a little about the times and about
the prevailing atmosphere that led a government to establish
such a comprehensive front-line defence early warning system.
Generations of British citizens born after 1945 have little idea of
how it feels to live in fear for the safety of their homes and
families. Few people born in Britain in the last few decades can
even guess at the terror engendered by the threat of war,
although it is a predicament in which many millions in other
parts of the world find themselves today. Even during the Cold
War years, when the world lay under the threat of nuclear war,
people did not in general rest uneasy in their beds. In 1925 it
was a completely different story, however. Europe had not long
emerged from the most devastating war it had ever seen, a war
that had almost walked onto the very doorstep of Britain.
During the Victorian age, the country had known a sense of
security that had enabled successive governments to send
troops all over the world, leaving British shores relatively
unguarded.

The First World War was like no previous war in a number
of quite startling ways. One of the most instantly recognizable
differences was the threat of air attack. Battles had always been
fought firmly on the ground, or at sea. Suddenly, there was a
third alternative. Initially the threat came not only from aircraft
but from Germany's huge airships, the terrifying zeppelins. The
targets of this new form of warfare were all too often civilian.
As well as fighting the Allied armies in the trenches, Germany
saw how she could cause panic and demoralization of the
public by attacking British cities and factories from the air.

Surprisingly, in spite of the aeroplane's awesome potential for causing devastation on a large scale, governments throughout the world were slow to realize it. The British Army saw the aeroplane purely as a means of reconnaissance, a way of observing enemy positions and troop movements. The main use for this information was to direct artillery with a greater degree of accuracy. In a bid to 'see over the hill' in front of them, the Royal Artillery had tried various schemes, including standing a gun limber on its end, thus making a high platform upon which an observer could sit. In the 1880s the Royal Engineers had used balloons for observation in both the Sudanese and Bechuanaland campaigns. In the 1899-1902 South African War, balloons had again been used to great effect, much to the frustration of the Boers, who considered that they gave an unfair advantage. But it was not until 1911 that the Royal Engineers were to form an Air Battalion. This consisted of one company of aeroplanes, one of small airships, one of balloons and one of man-lifting kites. Out of these the Royal Flying Corps was formed in 1912 as a joint service, with Naval and Military Wings. Britain had a clearly defined idea of the use of military aviation: it was for reconnaissance purposes, full stop. The Royal Navy, however, saw the potential in both aeroplanes and airships, since from their elevated position they would be able to survey the waters for many hundreds of miles, allowing the fleet to maintain a favourable tactical position, always keeping one step ahead of the enemy. The Army saw a similar role for these new machines. They would be able to observe enemy troop movements, fortifications, railheads, depots and dumps.

The Germans were also to establish naval and military corps of aviation, but they too were slow to see an aggressive role for their aeroplanes; indeed, the Army Air Service was placed under the command of the Inspector-General of Military Transport. Germany saw much greater potential in her huge airships. The first zeppelin made its trial flight as early as 1900, and by the outbreak of war in 1914, Germany had a considerable fleet of them, and a clear view of their destructive capabilities.

Italy was the first country to use an aircraft in actual warfare. In 1911 the Italians had used five aeroplanes in manoeuvres in Libya. Then, on 23 October 1911, during the war between Italy and Turkey, a certain Captain Piazza, the Commander of Italy's Air Fleet, took off on what was the very first war flight. The first bombing raid took place on 1 November 1911, when Lieutenant Cavotti dropped four modified grenades on Turkish troops. After this and other raids, Turkey protested strongly against the use of aeroplanes. Although they caused far less damage than either artillery or naval bombardments, it was obvious from the very start that aeroplanes and airships brought unparalleled terror to their victims.

A system for detecting and reporting the movements of enemy aircraft appeared in Britain as early as late 1914. Initially, this covered an area extending for 60 miles around London, within which the police were instructed to report to the Admiralty, by telephone, any sightings of aircraft or zeppelins. In 1915 this area was extended to cover East Anglia, Northamptonshire, Oxfordshire, Hampshire and the Isle of Wight.

The first direct attack on Britain for centuries took place on 21 December 1914, when a German seaplane bombed Dover, though both bombs happily fell short of the target and landed in the sea. The first bomb actually to explode on British soil did so on 24 December 1914, when another lone raider once again bombed Dover. These first isolated incidents showed that in what was, in fact, the dawning of aerial warfare, Britain was no longer the invulnerable island fortress. On 19 January 1915 the first zeppelin attacks were made, against Yarmouth and King's Lynn. Germany's confidence grew quickly and it wasn't long before raids were causing death and destruction nationwide, the targets as far afield as London, Hull and Tyneside. During the opening weeks of the war, the Germans took up a popular song directed against their now most hated adversary, England: *'Flieg, Zeppelin, Flieg, Hilf uns im Krieg, Fliege nach England, England wird abgebrannt, Zeppelin flieg.'* Roughly translated it means: 'Fly, Zeppelin, Fly, Help us in the war, Fly to England, England shall be destroyed by fire, Zeppelin, fly.'

The 19 January attack employed a total of three zeppelins, the L3, L4 and L6. L6 had engine trouble about halfway across the North Sea and had to return to her base at Nordholz. L3 crossed the Norfolk coast at Ingham just after eight in the evening, under the cover of rain and fog, and dropped six 110-pound bombs, plus incendiaries and parachute flares, on Yarmouth. Two people were killed and a further thirteen injured. After the raid, the L3 returned across the sea at roughly ten o'clock.

L4 crossed the English coast at around eight o'clock, at a point near Mundesley. She dropped two bombs on Sheringham and then made her way to King's Lynn, where she offloaded a further seven high-explosive and six incendiary bombs, killing two more people, one of them a child.

The first ever air raid on London happened on 31 May 1915. The zeppelin LZ38 dropped thirty grenades and eighty-nine incendiary bombs, which killed seven people and wounded thirty-five. Quite understandably, the terror caused by the zeppelins brought panic, and even riots, among British civilians. It was imperative that the home defences should be made stronger, and to that end Royal Flying Corps squadrons were either created or brought back from France to help protect against the raids. During the early stages of the war the RFC was mainly deployed on the Western Front, as Britain had been considered to be safe from attack. Now public disquiet – and anger against both the raiders and the authorities for apparently doing so little to protect lives and property – were so great that the air defence of the country became a matter of urgent priority.

In actual fact the early German raids caused very little damage. Zeppelins, for all the terror they inspired, were easy targets for the home defences, and a number were destroyed by aircraft or anti-aircraft fire. Moreover, they were easily deflected from their targets, and were at the mercy of bad weather. Their real value to the Germans was, first, that pilots, aircraft and anti-aircraft guns and their crews had to be diverted from the main effort in France to defend against them, and, second, the alarm they caused among the British public.

Posters were displayed throughout London in an effort to make the public themselves help in tracking the movements of enemy aircraft. Beneath the words 'PUBLIC WARNING' in large letters the posters showed silhouettes of German and British airships and aeroplanes, with a message which read:

The public are advised to familiarize themselves with the appearance of British and German Airships and Aeroplanes, so that they may not be alarmed by British aircraft, and may take shelter if German aircraft appear. Should hostile aircraft be seen, take shelter immediately in the nearest available house, preferably in the basement, and remain there until the aircraft have left the vicinity: do not stand about in crowds and do not touch unexploded bombs. In the event of hostile aircraft being seen in country districts, the nearest Naval, Military or Police Authorities should, if possible, be advised immediately by Telephone of the time of appearance, the direction of flight, and whether the aircraft is an airship or an aeroplane.

In 1917 it was decided that the system for detecting enemy aircraft was totally unsatisfactory. The War Office was given control of the situation and as the raids continued, new measures were implemented. 1917 was becoming a crucial year, for the whole nature of Germany's offensive against England was beginning to take ever more horrifying shape. On 13 June 1917, fourteen Gotha GIV twin-engined bombers made a raid against London. These new weapons were much more accurate and consequently devastating than the zeppelins of previous raids. On the 13 June raid alone, nearly 600 people were killed or injured. The terror was becoming ever more real.

The War Office placed all sections of the ground and air defences of London under the command of Major-General E. B. Ashmore, CB, CMG, MVO, the man who is popularly considered to be the founder of the Observer Corps. Ashmore's command was known as the London Air Defence Area (LADA), which comprised aerodromes, emergency landing-grounds, searchlights, gun stations, balloon aprons, and coastal and inland watching-posts. Within this scheme, Ashmore used to great effect all the existing defence units which covered the London area and districts to the south and south-east of the city.

Britain had adapted observation balloons originally used on the Western Front to form balloon aprons around London. There were three such aprons, each of which consisted of five balloons tethered in a line, supporting gigantic nets made of steel cable. The problem was that the weight of the nets was too great for the balloons to lift to a height great enough for maximum effectiveness. By the end of the war there were eight aprons in use around London; by then, several of the balloons were of greater gas capacity, thereby increasing the effectiveness of the barrage.

In some places, men equipped with binoculars were posted on high ground in areas which were known to be crossed by enemy aircraft. If an aeroplane approached they would ring up the police station and report it. One of the largest and most necessary undertakings of Ashmore's scheme was the work needed to establish a reliable telephone system. However, the work was not completed sufficiently to enable full operation until September 1918, which proved to be a little late, as the last German raids had taken place in May of that year. But although Ashmore's telephone network may have been completed a fraction too late, and after the Armistice was allowed rapidly to deteriorate, it was still to be resurrected in due course as the basis on which the Royal Observer Corps was formed.

The policy at the end of the First World War was to disband or demobilize vast sections of the country's defences. The government – indeed, most people – now considered that lasting peace was the order of the day, and believed that Europe would never again see another conflict of this nature. It had been the war to end all wars. Why, then, in 1925, was there a need to form the Observer Corps? The truth is that the new-found feelings of security were short-lived, and the public again began to worry about the safety of their homes. At that time France was seen by many as a potential enemy of the future. She possessed large military forces, and her closeness ensured that her aircraft could, with little difficulty, cross the Channel and bomb British cities. The population still remembered with fear their experiences of but a few short years before. A popular phrase of the time was, 'The bomber will always get through.' It had been coined by Air Marshal Sir Hugh Trenchard, the Chief of Air Staff, who had commanded the RFC for most of the war, and it made people at home very concerned about the situation, in which the French could field 600 aircraft, where the Royal Air Force could just about muster 40 actually based in Britain. New moves were afoot to create a better defensive structure, and in 1923 an Air Defence of Great Britain was authorised by the government. The main component of this plan was the creation of RAF squadrons to cover all vulnerable areas. The Observer Corps slipped into the proceedings through the persistence of Ashmore and a few other stalwarts.

Ashmore wanted to revitalize and improve the system that had come into operation in the very last stages of the war: essentially, to establish a network of manned observation posts which could report the movement of enemy aircraft to the nearest police station via the telephone links that had already been extensively designed. Permission was given for a series of experiments, to see whether or not the network would prove to be a useful part of home defence. The first of these experiments were carried out in August and September 1924 and took the form of aircraft tracking trials in the area between the Romney Marshes and Tonbridge. They proved to be very successful; in fact, so impressed was the government that in 1925 the go-ahead was given to form the first two observation areas. These were No 1 Group, with its headquarters in Maidstone, and No 2 Group with its headquarters in Horsham. They were able to cover an area embracing the whole of Kent and Sussex, and parts of Surrey. Within this area there were forty-three observation posts, twenty-seven of which belonged to Maidstone and sixteen to Horsham. As well as observation posts, the two groups were equipped with plotting centres where all the information could be channelled and processed. The personnel who manned the posts and centres were enrolled as special constables. The boundaries of these first groups coincided, where telephone exchanges permitted, with the boundaries of the county in which they were sited, Maidstone

Group, therefore, for the most part covering Kent, and Horsham Group Sussex. This county concept was the idea of the War Office, which controlled Home Defence at that time. Local control was given to the Chief Constable of the county – hence the reason why the first observers were all special constables.

At the very beginning, an Observer Corps post was exactly that – a post. The selected site would be beneath the nearest telephone pole, and a field telephone would be attached to the wire. The post itself would have no form of protection and would be completely exposed. There would be a tripod for the chart table and the 'Heath Robinson', a wooden instrument resembling an upended pantograph, used in conjunction with a separate vertical height bar.

Despite his successes, General Ashmore was still unhappy, and kept up the pressure to form further groups and carry out more tests. By the end of 1926 the Observer Corps covered an area from Hampshire to the middle of Suffolk. No 3 Group was formed at Winchester, followed by No 18 at Colchester, and Ashmore proposed more and more extensions to the area covered, such as Hertfordshire and Buckinghamshire. Even Harrow and Uxbridge were to receive their own observation posts.

The changing location of the Winchester group control room, as explained by Observer Commander A. B. Maasz and Observer Officer N. Parker in an *ROC Journal* article, is a good example of the improvised nature of the organization in the years before suitable premises were supplied. Initially, the control room occupied a tiny room in the post office. In 1927 it moved to a local store, and remained here for six years until it moved to the Blue Triangle Club, the local Young Women's Christian Association headquarters. Apparently disturbed by the frequent strains of dance music, the control room moved again, this time to a wooden-framed building on the post office roof which, as the Second World War approached, was protected by sandbags round the walls and extra corrugated iron on the roof.

As the Observer Corps grew bigger and bigger, it was decided to place it under the control of the Air Ministry, with effect from 1 January 1929. As it was now a corporate body, it was also decided to appoint a commanding officer. The very first Commandant of the Observer Corps was Air Commodore E. A. D. Masterman, CB, CMG, CBE, AFC, who took up his post on 1 March 1929, carrying out his duties directly under the command of Headquarters, Air Defence of Great Britain.

It would seem that the Corps had made a very good start. It had set off at a cracking pace, perhaps even too fast for, after being taken over by the Air Ministry, the pace began to slow to a virtual crawl. After five years in service, the Corps was to remain no larger than Ashmore's original four groups. Today, it is hard to understand why this should have been the case. It would seem that London and the surrounding area were considered to be the only places at risk in any future war; now that this select region was suitably covered, things came to a standstill. It may well have been that, having received its new status with the Air Ministry, the Corps lost a little of its pioneer spirit. Or perhaps the Commandant decided that it was better to spend time and money improving the existing system, rather than trying to enlarge an untested force – indeed, a force that might never have to be tested. Whatever the reasons behind this slowing-down phase, however, things did pick up slightly in 1931 with the creation of No 17 Group, with its centre at Watford.

By the mid-thirties, events were to take a dramatic turn. The political situation in Europe was worsening by the hour, driven by a Germany again growing in strength and aggression. One effect of this was that in January 1935 the Boyd Committee recommended that the Observer Corps should be expanded in four stages. New groups were to be formed, and by the Munich Crisis of 1938, most of the country was covered by a spider's web of Observer Corps posts, manned by volunteers, who were rewarded with the sum of 1s 3d for a working hour. In true volunteer style, most of the observers would not accept the money. They had volunteered, not to find a suitable wartime job, but from a sense of duty. In 1939 the monitoring posts were still unprotected and exposed, and it was at last understood that they required some sort of cover. Each post was given an allowance of £5 with which to provide suitable protection. There was no official building plan, and it was left up to the observers themselves to pull together and make the most of the situation. Quite often wooden sheds were erected as satellite posts, especially along the coastline. Many of these were without a plotting instrument, and the observers had to rely on guesswork. Even though the Corps had the country pretty much covered, there were still odd spots where the satellites came in handy. They could at least identify the type of aircraft and report it via their telephone link, so that the posts along the aeroplane's general flight-path were warned in advance.

When the Observer Corps was officially 'called out' on 24 August 1939, its network covered the whole of Great Britain and it could field a force of 40,000 trained watchers. At last all the hard work was to pay off. The foresight and determination of men like Ashmore now ensured that, as Europe once again

Observer R.T. Snow of Kingsworthy post standing in front of Hawker Hind of 49 Squadron during an OC visit to RAF Worthy Down 1937-1938. (ROCM/Tony Dowland)

descended into war, Britain at least had a reliable early warning system that could set the wheels of the home defence machine into operation.

At the time of being 'stood down' in 1991, the headquarters of the Royal Observer Corps was at RAF Bentley Priory, at Stanmore in Middlesex, which had become Observer Corps HQ in 1938, although its association with the Corps goes back to 1935, when it became Southern Area HQ. During the Second World War, Bentley Priory was destined to play a key role in the defence of Britain. By the time it came into contact with the Observer Corps it already had a long and proud history. The priory stands on a hill near the village of Stanmore and commands a spectacular view which encompasses nearly all of London – a position and view that proved very useful in the troubled years ahead.

There are a number of legends that associate the location with the Ancient British Queen of the Iceni, Boadicea, and much of the following information is drawn from research into the subject by Peter Shephard, Editor of the *ROC Journal*. One story suggests that the warrior queen is actually buried within the grounds. Following the defeat of her army at Stanmore in AD 61 by the Roman legions of Suetonius Paulinus, Boadicea committed suicide by taking poison. She had become queen of her tribe after the death of her husband, King Prasutagus, who had made an agreement with the Roman Emperor, Nero, that after he was dead Boadicea should be allowed to rule jointly with Rome. The Romans were pleased to come to such an arrangement, but after the death of Prasutagus, equally pleased to break their word. The kingdom of the Iceni was plundered, Boadicea was flogged and her daughters raped. Quite understandably, not only the Iceni, but also most of the neighbouring tribes were outraged by Rome's treachery. Boadicea became the head of a huge British army that set about taking its revenge on the Roman city of Colchester. In a devastating attack they almost totally destroyed the town, massacring nearly all of the inhabitants; later they burnt London and St Albans. Boadicea's next challenge was to face a well-trained and well-armed Roman legion, the 9th, under the command of Petilius Cerialis. The Roman infantry was annihilated to the very last man, but Cerialis managed to escape from the battlefield and send word to Suetonius Paulinus, who was fighting with his own legions in the mountains of Wales.

As Boadicea marched south towards London, Paulinus hurried to intercept her. The two armies clashed at Stanmore and a terrible battle ensued, which cost the lives of 80,000 Britons, though, remarkably, only 1,000 Romans. Many places in England claim to be the site of Boadicea's last battle, but the facts are very uncertain; however, Bentley Priory's claim to be her final resting-place is as favourable as any. The original priory was probably built on a site that was already sacred to the ancient Britons, for the first Christian establishments quite often coincided with earlier centres of pagan worship. It was the tradition of the Iceni to bury their leaders in holy ground on a hill, and *Beonet/leah,* meaning coarse grass upland, may well be the earliest form of the word Bentley.

A priory was first established on the site in the twelfth century. In 1543 it was granted to Sir Thomas Cranmer, who handed it over to Henry VIII in exchange for land at Wimbledon, thus ending its religious employment. Most of it, as it appears today, was built by James Duberley, who acquired the estate in 1766, and the buildings were designed by the renowned architect Sir John Soane. In the late eighteenth century, and for some time afterwards, it became something of a social and political centre. Owned by John Hamilton, Marquess of Abercorn, it was visited by the grand and the famous, among them statesmen such as Pitt, Wellington and Canning, and poets like Wordsworth and Moore.

In 1926 the Air Ministry purchased the Priory and forty acres of land. Its association with the Observer Corps, as already stated, began in 1935, when it became Southern Area HQ, and in 1938 it became the Corps' overall HQ. It was from Bentley Priory that Air Chief Marshal Sir Hugh Dowding, Commander-in-Chief of Fighter Command, later to become Lord Dowding of Bentley Priory, was to conduct the Battle of Britain.

Dowding arrived at Bentley Priory at 9 a.m. on 14 July 1936.

In establishing there the headquarters of Fighter Command, he began the task of creating an intricate defence organization. His plans were to merge all the elements available to him for use in the defence of the British Isles. Fighter squadrons, Anti-Aircraft Command, Balloon Command, RDF stations and, of course, the Observer Corps, were all vital cogs in his machine. So Bentley Priory became the Observer Corps headquarters, and the adjacent Glenthorn House became the headquarters of Anti-Aircraft Command. In January 1939 excavations began for the underground operations block, which became operational on 9 March 1940.

CHAPTER TWO
At the Outbreak of the Second World War

When war came on 3 September 1939, the Commandant of the Observer Corps was Air Commodore A. D. Warrington-Morris, CMG, OBE, who had taken over from Masterman on 1 March 1936. The men who manned the observation posts in the years that led up to the outbreak of war were part-time observers who gave up a great deal of their leisure to watch and listen for aircraft in preparation for any future threat to the country. Although they provided what ultimately became a crucial service, they were not always looked upon with due respect by members of the public. In fact, as war seemed more and more imminent, they came to be regarded as eccentric, overgrown school boys who liked to play at war. As it turned out, they were to win the admiration and respect of the entire country for their unending and untiring devotion to duty. Without the Observer Corps and radar, acting as the nation's eyes and ears, it can honestly be said that the work of the fighter aircraft, anti-aircraft guns, searchlights and balloon barrages would have been based largely on guesswork. No German aircraft could cross the British coastline by day or night without being seen or heard. From the moment it crossed over the coast it was detected and monitored. Its height and direction was always known. No matter what altitude it adopted, or how erratic a course it steered, it remained well and truly observed.

As soon as an aircraft came into view and was identified as an enemy, the observation post would report its height, direction, nationality and type to the area centre via its direct telephone link. In turn, the area centre would pass the necessary information to a Fighter Command sector operations room. Sector would then process this information to alert the various other parts of the air defence system – fighter stations, anti-aircraft gun positions, searchlight and balloon units, police and fire brigades. All the observation posts had been built in positions on high ground from where they could command an uninterrupted view for as far as possible. The most important job of a post was to identify the aircraft in the first place. So each observer had to know not only how to recognise both enemy and friendly aircraft by sight, but also if possible, by distinguishing different engine sounds. This was particularly useful at night, for observation had to be maintained round the clock. Whether or not the identification of aircraft by sound alone was reliable, however, remains a matter of controversy. In fact, the Germans did not synchronise the engines of their multi-engined aircraft, as the British did, giving them a characteristic and distinctive engine note. Furthermore, the Luftwaffe's only four-engined bomber, the FW Kondor, was rarely employed over Britain. Hence identification by sound, to someone really well-trained and experienced, might have been easier than at first appears.

Having observed and reported the presence of the enemy aircraft, the posts maintained their reports until it was well out of sight. By this time the area centre would already be receiving information about the aeroplane from the next observation post on its flight path. The enemy plane would be plotted in this fashion until such time as it turned away or had been shot down by one of the defences.

From their lonely posts the observers could provide a wide range of other useful services to the authorities, such as the reporting of fires, black-out offences, suspicious acts, or where and when bombs had been dropped. They could also report on the progress of aerial battles and, at times, give the location of a crashed aircraft. They could even pinpoint the position of any airmen who had baled out of their cockpits. All in all, the job was hardly dull, and grew in importance as the war progressed.

At an area centre, most of the space was dominated by a very large table covered by a chart of the area that the centre plotted. The chart was sub-divided into hundreds of small numbered squares. A group of men wearing headphones sat around the table. These men, called plotters, were in direct communication with the posts, and through his earphones each plotter could listen to reports coming in from three of the posts in the area. Having received a report from one of his posts, the plotter would place a coloured counter onto the appropriate square on the chart. As the reports from the post progressed, following the changing position of the aircraft, the plotter would move the counter from square to square to give an exact location, as well as showing the aircraft's course and speed. The plotter would go on doing this until the aircraft had either been shot down or had left the area covered by the chart. If the aircraft had not been shot down by the time it left the area, it would undoubtedly have already been picked up by the next group of posts and plotted by their area centre.

Above the plotters, sitting on a raised platform around the room, sat another group of men, the tellers. From their elevated positions they had a comprehensive view over the entire area. It was the teller who would report the movements of all aircraft to the sector controller at Fighter Command, for broadcasting to the other defence centres and, in particular, to the fighter groups, so that they could scramble and intercept the approaching enemy. On occasions, however, the direct telephone lines between the posts and centres were inoperative. When this happened, the observers in the post would have to find an alternative method of reporting, usually either by finding the nearest telephone box, or by knocking on someone's door and using their telephone. Since many of the posts were built in remote places, this could be quite a challenge, especially given that reports had to be continuously maintained. It could mean an awful lot of running or cycling back and forth between post and telephone for some poor observer.

There were basically two types of observer, known as A and B members. The A members worked a forty-eight-hour week, which was generally split up into six days of eight hours each. The B members were part-timers and gave whatever service they could during evenings or at weekends. All observers, whether A or B, received thorough training to make them experts in aircraft identification.

At the beginning of the war the observers had still not been issued with uniforms; instead, they wore civilian clothes but with a striped armband bearing the words 'Observer Corps.' They were also issued with a black beret to which was fixed the corps' badge which, of course, depicted a beacon-lighter from the days of Queen Elizabeth I, with the motto 'Forewarned is Forearmed.' Steel helmets, often with the letters 'OC' painted on the front, could also be worn.

There were usually two observers manning a post at any one time. One, wearing headphones and with a mouthpiece strapped over his chest, reported the movements of aircraft directly to the plotter at the chart table in the area centre. The second observer operated the post plotter, which stood on a tripod in the middle of the post. This primarily consisted of a round dial, which was marked to correspond with a section of the big chart at the area centre (its design was credited to an Engineer Captain Ball, who had been the head observer at the Exbury post in Winchester Group). All spotters were also equipped with a pair of powerful binoculars. Some, though not all, posts were, by local arrangement, connected by a buzzer system to factories or other places of work or education, and could thus warn the occupants to head for the safety of the nearest air-raid shelter. A typical message from a post observer to his relevant area centre might have run: 'Five Me109s approaching Watford at 10,000 feet, flying north-west.' All aircraft had to be reported, whether enemy or, as was more often the case during the early months of the war, friendly.

An observer in those long-gone days needed to possess a huge amount of dedication. The fact of the matter was that life at a post could be extremely uncomfortable. The majority were built on legs and resembled the crow's nest on a ship. Quite often the posts were in very remote locations, and were frequently extremely exposed. It wasn't unknown for the Observer Corps to site posts on the top of water towers, church towers, multi-storey and similar high buildings. Because observers on duty had to maintain their vigil at all times, they were unable to seek any form of shelter – they had to stay alert and awake at their post throughout their watch, and regardless of the often atrocious weather. As can be imagined, it was a pretty tough existence. The posts were generally protected by sandbags and quite often had a room beneath them which served as a bedroom or kitchen. This, however, could only be used by observers who were off duty, or if there were more than two observers at the post.

Every post had to maintain a log, in which was recorded everything that happened during a particular watch. During the first part of the war, log books made dull reading. However, as the months rolled by and Germany began to mount its air offensive, the story was to change dramatically.

The first Nazi bombs to fall on British soil did so during a German air raid on the Shetland Islands on 13 November 1939 (although during a raid on the Firth of Forth on 16 October, bombs had fallen into the water, these were the first bombs actually to fall on land). On 17 November, according to *Hutchinsons's Pictorial History of the War:* 'An enemy plane, apparently a Heinkel reconnaissance machine, flies over Lancashire and Cheshire and is detected by the Royal Air Force Observer Corps. No bombs are dropped and it is driven off.' In the months ahead Observer Corps sightings became too frequent to warrant such mention.

Also in November of 1939, the Observer Corps featured in a statement made by Sir Kingsley Wood, Secretary of State for Air:

We have been able to satisfy ourselves by actual operations that the various elements of our air defences, the anti-aircraft guns and searchlights, the fighter squadrons, the balloon barrages for close defence, and the units of the Observer Corps, have been successfully welded into an efficient and adaptable system under the operational control and command of one commander-in-chief. This system of unified control, the strength of which is steadily increasing, has justified our expectations and gives us the great advantage that our whole defence organization can thus be adapted and adjusted to meet the exigencies and requirements of any particular moment and circumstance. In this great organization every element is manfully playing its part. The Territorial units manning the guns and searchlights and, by no means least, if I may single them out for special mention, the personnel of the balloon barrage and of the Observer Corps. They have had to keep their constant watch with little excitement through the long hours of waiting for the sight or sound of an enemy machine. Many of them are stationed at remote places, and many have had to carry out their duties in difficult conditions. But we know that we can fully rely upon them to carry them out, uneventful though they may be, with efficiency and uncomplaining spirit.

On 9 January 1940, the Prime Minister, Neville Chamberlain, made a speech at the Mansion House in which he sought to show the country how the armed forces had been developing during the early months of the war. He also brought a great deal of attention to the development of the civil defences. The speech underlines how, more and more, the Observer Corps was becoming a crucial part of a much larger chain of defences:

Parallel with this development of our military forces we have the great system of civil defence which has been built up by way of preparation against air raids. Day and night our fighter aircraft, our anti-aircraft guns, our balloons and Observer Corps are mobilised and stand ready to detect and meet the raiders. Then we have also the auxiliary firemen and police, the air-raid wardens, the casualty services, and all the great army of volunteers, most of them part-time, unpaid workers, who form an essential part of our system of defence. Then, finally, there are the safety measures which we have taken to diminish risks, evacuation, the black-out, the restrictions upon the hours of places of public entertainment, and all the complicated arrangements for casualties, first-aid posts, and hospitals. These vast preparations, and they have occasioned a good deal of hardship, inconvenience, loss of money, and, I am afraid, loss of life in street accidents, and then, after all, four months have gone by and the air raids have not come. Some people think it really is very disappointing, and it is not surprising that others should ask whether, after all, all these things were necessary, and whether we had not gone a good deal too far in the direction of safety. Well, I wish I could take that view.

By February, although the air war was still extremely quiet, the Observer Corps had already gained a reputation of efficiency. Once again, the Secretary of State for Air praised the corps' efforts:

I would like to commend the work of our Civil Defence Forces. Like the Observer Corps, for months now men and women who have joined the Ambulance, ARP, Fire Brigade, and other organizations have been engaged in our many considerable preparations against air attack. This is vital work. Because attacks have not as yet been made, it does not mean that anyone should relax for a moment. When the call comes everyone must be prepared and ready, and all that has been done will, I have no doubt, be abundantly justified in the great assistance this work will give to the defences of our country.

An article by J. B. Priestley, published in the *News Chronicle* on 17 October 1939, gives a good insight into the Observer Corps at the very onset of the Second World War. In describing the observers, he wrote:

You can divide them into two classes, the indoor and the outdoor. I was taken first to see the indoor men at work. The place looks like some new kind of gambling hell. Twelve of them sit round a large table, and across this table they keep moving halma men and different-coloured counters. And when they speak, they have the quiet and rather monotonous voices of croupiers. But they are speaking into telephones and they are wearing earphones. They are the plotters. Above them, with a clear view of the whole table, sit the tellers, who are recording everything and also using telephones. Just outside is a man working a teleprinter. Altogether there are between twenty and thirty men operating this centre at any one shift, but as it never stops functioning, day and night, there are, of course, several shifts and nearly two hundred members of the Observer Corps doing duty there. They are collecting, recording and passing on the reports of the outside observers. They know the course and height of every plane moving in this part of the world. The halma men and coloured counters tell an instant tale. This is not a game, though you could play it as a game. It is part, and a very essential part, of the defence of Britain against bombing raids. At the end of some of those telephones are units of the Royal Air Force waiting to engage the new armadas of the sky.

According to the *Concise Oxford Dictionary*, halma is 'a game played by two or four persons on a board of two hundred and fifty-six squares, with men advancing from one corner to the opposite corner by being moved over other men into vacant squares.' Although the task of the Observer Corps was far from being a game, it is refreshing to read this jovial tribute, written during what must have been a deadly serious time.

Referring to the observers who occupied the posts, Priestley continued:

On the top of a hill a few miles away I met an insurance agent and a radio salesman, wearing badges and armlets, their oldest clothes and huge smiles. Theirs is a job that would drive schoolboys mad with envy. Any healthy-minded lad would give all his pocket-money to take a turn at this observation post, with its sandbagged watching place, its dug-out and camouflaged hut. Here is sentry work of a new and exciting kind. You are warned by telephone of the approach of an aircraft, with some reference to direction and height. In daylight your instrument enables you to keep the aircraft in view across your bit of the sky and to plot accurately its direction. Meanwhile, your mate is telephoning back to the centre the results of your observation. At night sound must replace sight, but the work goes on just the same. If and when raiding begins on any considerable scale, this job will be terrifically exciting. But even up to now it has not been entirely boring, for practices are frequent, to keep everybody interested and alert and to give the observers the necessary experience.

In his final summary, Priestley touched on the comradeship of the observers in these early days of the war:

And another thing. Although at a first glance this observing may seem so much games and fun, actually it is no joke to keep your business or profession going in these days and at the same time turn out at all hours, for spells of duty on the hill or round the plotting table. But these fellows are not only doing it, but are doing it in fine comradely style. Indeed, the whole working and organization of this Observer Corps, which seemed to me to have a spirit at once efficient, comradely, genial, appeared to me absolutely first class in both conception and execution. If I knew who planned it all, I would hand him the biggest bouquet of adjectives I could find.

General Ashmore would undoubtedly have been delighted to receive such praise. More than that, however, Priestley's article gives a fine impression of the spirit and atmosphere of the corps as it prepared to meet its biggest challenge.

Post observers around the wooden tripod at Dorchester post, at the start of the Second World War. (ROCM/Obs Lt John Norman)

Group Captain Sir Hugh Dundas
CBE DSO DFC DL

Those of us who were lucky enough to serve as pilots in Fighter Command in the early part of Hitler's war, when the British Isles were under constant and fierce attack by the Luftwaffe, know better than most how much is owed to the Royal Observer Corps and its tireless and devoted members. Winter, spring, summer and autumn, day and night, fair weather and foul, they were out there, supplementing the fragile aircraft recognition and tracking system provided by a brand new and still only partly developed technology with a vast nation-wide network of expert human spotters. Thanks to them, many a raider was intercepted before reaching its target. And thanks to them, also, many a young Spitfire and Hurricane pilot was helped safely home, in the dark or in bad weather, at a time when navigational aids, now taken for granted, were virtually non-existent.

The work done so successfully by the Royal Observer Corps was a vital factor in winning the Battle of Britain and so averting invasion and the occupation of our land. I salute the Corps and all who served in it.

Hugh Dundas.

Above: His Majesty The King visits an Observer Corps post during a two-day tour of Eastern Command in 1940. (Virtue & Co Ltd) **Below left:** A wartime scene at No 1 Group Maidstone Centre showing both table and balcony being manned. (ROCM/Fred Nye) **Below right:** Group Captain Sir Hugh Dundas. (The Yorkshire Post)

CHAPTER THREE
The Battle of Britain

The Battle of Britain, which is generally taken to have lasted from 10 July to 12 October 1940, proved to be the greatest test of the Observer Corps' efficiency. How well the organization did its job, and the respect it gained, can be measured by the fact that on 9 April 1941, it was announced in the House of Commons that His Majesty King George VI had granted the corps permission to use the style and title 'Royal'.

Before the Battle of Britain started in earnest, science had enabled Britain to develop a new system of aircraft detection which came to be known as radar. In 1935 a group of eminent scientists had been asked to set up an Aeronautical Research Committee. In view of Germany's increased development of aircraft, especially in the bomber field, their brief was to look at different ways of repelling an air attack. Amusingly, as it seems nowadays, one of the possibilities that the scientists looked into was the use of a 'Death Ray' that would destroy approaching aircraft. Equally amusingly, when they presented the idea to Robert Watson-Watt of the Radio Department of the National Physical Laboratory, he informed them that it was complete nonsense. It must have been quite an interesting moment when the brainiest men in the kingdom were told by Watson-Watt that they were a bunch of crackpots. However, on considering the idea, it was found that approaching aircraft re-radiated radio signals, a discovery that led to the invention of radar.

Although the Observer Corps was responsible for tracking the movements of aircraft over land, it was, unfortunately, unable to begin observations until the aircraft had actually reached the coast. They had no means of detecting the approach of aircraft from across the Channel, so that even though all aircraft were monitored from the moment they appeared in British skies, defences could not be prepared in advance, nor squadrons scrambled. Radar, however, changed everything, for it made it possible to detect the presence of an aircraft from up to 100 miles away. This detection, although unable to identify the nature of the aircraft, was used as a form of early warning of the approach of possible hostile aircraft. By combining the radar tracks produced over the sea and the Observer Corps tracks made over land, the fighter controllers at RAF sector control rooms were able to build up a more comprehensive picture of enemy incursions, with the result that a much greater number of interceptions was attained.

'Radar' (RAdio Detection and Ranging) is an American word. The English system was originally known as RDF (Radio Direction-Finding) or, later 'radio location', and the word 'radar' was not adopted by the Royal Air Force until 1943. Thus, during the Battle of Britain the system was always referred to as RDF. By the start of the war, a number of RDF stations had been built around the coast, stretching from Southampton to Tyneside. This RDF network was known as Chain Home.

For the purposes of air defence, Britain was divided into four

Painting of Kingsworthy post by Obs G.P. Kingdon, September 1940. (ROCM)

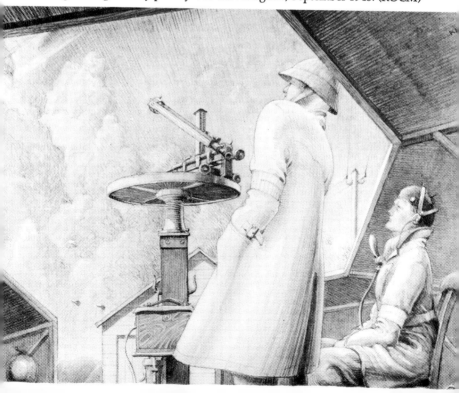

Fighter Command Groups. No 13 Group (Air Vice-Marshal Richard Saul) covered Scotland and the north of England from a line above Church Fenton. No 12 Group (Air Vice-Marshal Trafford Leigh-Mallory) covered the Midlands and most of Wales, reaching as far south as Duxford. No 10 Group (Air Vice-Marshal Sir Quintin Brand) covered South Wales and the west of England, stretching from Land's End to Middle Wallop. Finally, No 11 Group (Air Vice-Marshal Keith Park), which was to bear most of the German raids throughout the battle, covered the City of London and an area reaching southwards to the Isle of Wight and eastwards to the coast. Fighter Command Headquarters for the battle was at RAF Bentley Priory, Stanmore, which, as we have already seen, was also Observer Corps HQ. Each of the four Groups had its own headquarters: No 13 at Newcastle; No 12 at Watnall; No 10 at Box; and No 11 at Uxbridge. Information received from high-level and low-level radar stations around the coast, and from Observer Corps area centres, was simultaneously broadcast to sector stations. Sector stations would alert the fighter bases, enabling them to scramble their squadrons to intercept the enemy aircraft. No 13 Group had sector stations at Turnhouse, Acklington, Usworth and Church Fenton; No 12 Group at Kirton-in-Lindsey, Digby, Wittering, Duxford and Debden; No 10 Group at Filton and Middle Wallop; and No 11 Group at North Weald, Hornchurch, Biggin Hill, Kenley and Tangmere.

Tellers at Observer Corps area centres would pass their plots to a maximum of six Fighter Command sectors. At each of the Group HQs an Observer Corps liaison officer would be on duty to help filter the information as it came in. Even though Bentley Priory acted as Fighter Command's HQ and had its own operations room, the main ops room for No 11 Group, at Uxbridge, was considered to be the nerve centre of the battle. Here a huge 'tote board' displayed the precise state of readiness of the fighter squadrons, sector by sector.

Each sector operations room was presided over by a controller. In front of him would be a large map table where information received from the Observer Corps and the RDF stations was displayed by means of various symbols. A sector controller would thus be able to build up a complete picture of the progress of any raid and would also be able to see the condition and availability of the fighter squadrons within his sector. He would know exactly their state of readiness and, if a squadron was in the air, he would also be immediately aware of its location. In this way he would be able to conduct the movements of all his available aircraft against the raiders. He would also have information concerning the weather and cloud conditions readily at hand.

The squadrons themselves were sited at sector aerodromes. No 10 Group had airfields at Middle Wallop, Filton, Exeter, Pembrey, St Eval, Aston Down, Sutton Bridge and Hawarden. No 11 Group had airfields at Northolt, Kenley, Hawkinge, Biggin Hill, Gravesend, North Weald, Hornchurch, Tangmere, Southend, Manston, Croydon, and Hendon. No 12 Group had airfields at Debden, Martlesham, Duxford, Wittering, Digby, Kirton-in-Lindsey, and Coltishall. No 13 Group's airfields were at Catterick, Church Fenton, Leconfield, Usworth, Turnhouse, Drem, Grangemouth, Wick, Castletown, Dyce, Montrose and Acklington.

The RAF squadrons employed various states of readiness, the most relaxed of which was 'released'. If a squadron was released then its time was very much its own, since it was not expected to be in operation until a specified hour. In the meantime, the personnel could undertake routine maintenance or training flights, or play games and generally relax. If it was known for certain how long the release period would last, they would even be allowed to leave the station. The next state was 'available', which meant that the squadron members must be ready to spring into action, fully equipped and prepared. 'Readiness' was a similar state, but pilots were given a certain time-scale in which they would have to be airborne – normally a matter of minutes – and all personnel concerned had to stay close to their aircraft. During 'stand-by' pilots actually had to sit in their aircraft, with the engine switched off, but ready to take off immediately on receiving instructions from the sector controller.

The sector controller issued his orders based on his study of the operations room map. He would put enough aircraft into the air to intercept raiders, or to cover vulnerable points. He would not want to waste his resources by sending aircraft out unnecessarily, but at the same time it was his duty to keep a constant watch on those resources. He would have to know, for instance, whether aircraft were being refuelled, and therefore vulnerable to attack. Using the comprehensive tracks available to him, the controller's main task was to direct the fighters until they engaged the enemy. At this point, once the pilot had transmitted his 'tally-ho' message, the battle was left very much in the pilot's own hands. However, the controller was still able to contact pilots by radio-telephone, and dictate their actions if he saw fit. This might happen if a new wave of raiders had appeared on his map and it looked as though they were heading for a vulnerable area. It is easily seen, then, how important was the continued receipt of information from the Observer Corps, even during the course of a battle.

In many ways, the presence of the controller conformed an aerial battle more along the lines of a conventional ground encounter. For instance, every day controllers would hold a conference to discuss what had been learned and how this information could be used to out-think the enemy. Without the system of central control no battle, in the proper sense of the word, would have ever taken place. Without the information coming through to sector from the Observer Corps, the Royal Air Force would have been flying blind and, in most cases, either confronting an enemy who presented them with over-whelming numbers, or failing to find the enemy aircraft at all.

Of course, the fighter squadrons were not the only element of the defences that benefited from information sent, via the sector controller, by the Observer Corps. There were also the balloon barrages and the anti-aircraft batteries. The purpose of the balloon barrage around Britain was to prevent the enemy from making low-level bombing raids over vulnerable areas, and it was considered to be one of the most effective weapons against Nazi air attack. The balloons forced the raiders to fly at the heights at which they could be engaged by anti-aircraft guns and fighter aircraft. A steel cable attached to each balloon led to a winch on a lorry, and any aircraft that ventured into this cable would almost certainly be destroyed. The balloons were tethered in line about 100 yards apart, at heights up to several thousand feet, which meant that an enemy bomber flying at speed below the barrage had about a three-to-one chance of crashing into a cable. Once the pilot was forced to fly above the balloons he would come into range of the searchlights and so be a target for the ground defences, which could not deal effectively with aircraft flying at only a few hundred feet. Most of the balloon barrages were operated by men of the Auxiliary Air Force and covered not only London but other vulnerable points and populous areas in the provinces, particularly industrial and shipping centres. A barrage balloon was also mobile, and so could easily be moved from one location to another. When German aircraft began dropping magnetic mines from the air into the shipping channels around the east coast, a barrage was quickly erected in the area. Many of the balloons were flown from river barges and lighters and at once proved an effective defence against the low-flying mine-laying aircraft.

The balloons were, however, equally capable of destroying British aeroplanes, and their deployment therefore had to be strictly controlled, using the latest radar and Observer Corps information. RAF fighter pilots had to be fully aware of the balloons' operational status and locations. As the barrages were mobile, this was often a difficult task, and there were instances of our own aircraft falling foul of the deadly cables.

Some of the anti-aircraft and searchlight batteries were equipped with sound-locators, which were very useful pieces of equipment, and greatly aided their efficiency. Sound-locators looked rather like kettle drums fixed on a movable mounting; when pointed skywards, they could amplify the sound of an approaching enemy, and so give an idea of distance and position. Women of the Auxiliary Territorial Service (later superseded by the – also now defunct – Women's Royal Army Corps) provided their own observation service, and were often stationed at anti-aircraft gun sites where they operated predictors, range-finders and other instruments. The ATS engaged in these duties became known as 'air sentries'. At night, vision predictors could be used on targets illuminated by searchlights, and the ATS also operated kine-theodolites, which recorded shell-bursts. They also kept film records of anti-aircraft fire, which were used for training AA gunners. Heavy anti-aircraft gun batteries had height indicators – rather like huge telescopes, their calculations governed the actions of the big guns they served. The men who operated these machines were recruited from among university graduates, teachers, and the like.

The anti-aircraft batteries in the British Isles played a much greater role than they are often given credit for. In the twelve months ending on 31 December 1940, they shot down a total of 444½ enemy aircraft, the odd half representing the AA gunners' share in an enemy bomber which was finished off by RAF fighters after it had been 'winged' by a near miss from a ground battery.

Three hundred and thirty-four of those aircraft had been brought down since 1 September, a daily average of close to three, and it seemed that the batteries were equally successful by day or night. The number of destroyed German aircraft was probably many more than this, as the figure did not include aircraft that were so disabled or damaged by gunfire as to have been unable to reach their bases, or to have been written off having limped back.

On three occasions during 1940, Britain's AA gunners shot down more than fifty enemy aircraft in a week, and on one memorable occasion, the weekly score reached seventy. Their most successful twenty-four hours of the year was on 15 August. On that day alone, the gunners destroyed twenty-three enemy aircraft, a record bag contributed to by batteries as far apart as Dundee and Dover. In 1918 an aircraft flying at a height of 8,000 feet was virtually out of the reach of anti-aircraft batteries. The average height of the German aircraft brought down in the Second World War was 16,000 feet. Instead of flying at between 90 and 100 miles per hour, as bombers did in 1918, the speed of the Nazi raiders was often of the order of 250 miles per hour.

A system for giving 'imminent-danger' warnings to factories on war work was also introduced at this time. Air-raid warning officers were employed in Observer Corps area centres by the Ministry of Home Security, to alert certain crucial industrial centres. This scheme was responsible for saving millions of man-hours, and made a vital contribution to the production of a large bomber force and other war materials which, in the end, made possible the Allied invasion of Europe in 1944.

On 5 September 1940, Winston Churchill, who had succeeded Chamberlain as Prime Minister in May, gave the House of Commons a general review of the war. A point not yet touched upon in any depth in this narrative is the air-raid warning system. As well as the warnings that certain industrial works received directly from the Observer Corps, it can also be safely assumed that the majority of air-raid warnings sounded at this time were based on information processed from the various early warning systems, notably the Observer Corps. Churchill's own words give a good summary of the state of the warning system, and show that although civil defence organizations like the Observer Corps were gaining the nation's respect, the air-raid warning system in general was a matter of great concern. It appears to have been a case of one bad apple in the bunch – or, at least, at a time when everyone was commending the civil defence network, it is a surprise to uncover such criticism:

In the light of what we have learned so far with regard to the arrangements for air-raid warnings we have come to the conclusion that the arrangements for air-raid warnings, and what is to be done when they are given, which appears to be another question, require very considerable changes. There is no good sense in having these prolonged banshee howlings from sirens, two or three times a day over wide areas, simply because hostile aircraft are flying to or from some target which no one can know or even guess. All our precautions regulations have hitherto been based on this siren call, and I must say that one must admire the ingenuity of those who devised it as a means of spreading alarm. Indeed, most people now see how very wise Ulysses was when he stopped the ears of his sailors to all siren songs and had himself tied firmly to the mast of duty.

Now that we are settling down to the job we must have different arrangements from those devised before the war. It is right that every one should now know that the red warning is more in the nature of a general 'alert' than a warning of the imminence of danger to any particular locality. In many cases it is physically impossible to give the alarm before the attack. Constant alarms come to be something in the nature of no alarm, yet while they give no protection to very great numbers of people who take no notice of them, they undoubtedly exercise a disturbing effect upon necessary war work. All our regulations and much preaching have taught people that they should take a whole series of steps, mostly of a downward character, when they hear the siren sound, but it is no use having official regulations which require and enjoin immediate respect for the alarm, while exhortations are given, unofficially or officially, to disregard them and go on working.

In our own case today it was felt that the red warning should be taken merely as an 'alert', but that if special circumstances indicated the proximity of danger, then the condition of alarm should supervene. That is exactly what we did on receiving information that there was danger of a particular kind in the vicinity, and when that special condition departed we immediately resumed our work under the conditions of 'alert', until the 'All Clear', which had now sounded, restored us to normal.

Something like this unrehearsed experiment may well give us guidance in our future treatment of the problem. All our regulations require to be shaped to the new basis which is being established by actual contact with events.

What we want is the greatest measure of real warning that is compatible with what all our people are resolved upon, namely, the active maintenance of war production.

The job of sounding the warnings fell on the Air Raid Precautions (ARP) Department of the Home Office, but the decision to order air-raid warnings rested with the Air Officer

Commanding-in-Chief, Fighter Command, and was based on the Observer Corps and RDF tracks available to him. Initially, if possible, a preliminary alert, 'Yellow', warning of a possible raid by enemy aircraft, would be issued to police headquarters and to the control centre of the ARP in the district concerned.

The ARP controller could summon his staff into action at the press of a button. The message would be passed by telephone to the ARP wardens' posts, and Intelligence officers would mark all movements on maps with coloured pins. What were considered to be the four vital services, telephone, gas, water and electricity, had their own officers, who would be alerted ready to pass on to the authorities any problems.

If the raiders continued on the same course, Fighter Command would issue the 'Red' warning, which was the signal for the sounding of sirens and for individual wardens and police to take up their posts. Report centres were established, at which the wardens or police were to report emergencies. The report centre would pass this information on to the control centre, and from there ARP depots were alerted to respond to the threat.

By November 1940 the problem of factories engaged in war work which were losing vital hours needlessly because of the frequency of the sirens, had resulted in a number of practical suggestions, foremost among which was the use of roof-watchers. The idea was based very much along the same lines as the Observer Corps, only instead of reporting their observations to the national defence network, the roof-watchers were employed to warn their particular factories or premises. The Observer Corps would already have reported the approach of enemy aircraft, and the latter's movements would be tracked. Fighter Command would have already issued its relevant warning. So the decision whether or not to give an alert in a specific war-work location, would depend upon the best judgement of the roof-watchers themselves, who were trained as far as possible in aircraft recognition, and were equipped with powerful binoculars. Ernest Bevin, Minister of Labour and National Service, stated:

We have asked industry to carry on during air raids. We

suggested the system of roof-watchers. We do not limit our suggestion to this. You have a great ingenuity and you must have other ideas to achieve the same object, and that is not the only thing that can be done. I would say to the managements of the great undertakings it is your duty to devise every possible means for the safety of the work people in order to help them carry on. It is necessary to protect them from such dangers as falling glass and blast. This is not a thing to argue about, it is a thing to be done.

On 22 June 1940 France accepted an armistice with Germany. Hostilities on the Continent came to an end, with Europe largely in the grip of the Nazis. With the defeats of Norway, Belgium, Holland and France complete, Britain now stood alone against Hitler's military might. Germany's massive air attack on Britain was code-named 'Operation Attack of the Eagles', and the intended invasion was code-named 'Operation Sealion'. Although the country braced itself for the imminent air onslaught that would precede an invasion, the population became imbued with a stern resolve, everyone pulling together to strengthen England's defences against the enemy. There was a feeling of defiance, even cheerfulness, among the nation that has become familiar to us through television programmes, films and books. It would appear that in the face of Britain's greatest ever threat, her people discovered their greatest ever unity.

Initially, the Luftwaffe, which was commanded by Reichsmarshall Hermann Goering, sent small numbers of aircraft across the Channel to test the defences. These bombed airfields and coastal convoys, and also dive-bombed the RDF stations, the lofty towers of which stood out like sore thumbs. Although the raiders often hit the target, in most cases the RDF stations were operational again by the following morning. Unfortunately, however, the German fighters soon showed themselves to be superior to the British Boulton & Paul Defiants, with which a number of fighter squadrons were equipped. The Defiant was a two-seat fighter which had a power-operated turret mounting four rifle-calibre machine guns immediately behind the pilot's cockpit, instead of the more usual wing-mounted (and, in some cases, fuselage-mounted) machine-guns. The disadvantages of such a layout had been learned quite early on in the First World War. Although the Defiant was a clean design, and was powered by the same Rolls-Royce Merlin engine as the Hurricane and Spitfire, it was outclassed in every respect – speed, ceiling, manoeuvrability, fire-power – while the turret-gunner was plagued by blind-spots. Luckily, more and more squadrons were being equipped with Spitfires and Hurricanes. By 31 July 1940, Britain had a network of thirty-nine fighter stations, occupied by sixty-six squadrons. Only two squadrons still relied on Defiants, the others being equipped with Spitfires, Hurricanes and Blenheims, or a combination of these aircraft. The predominating type was the Hurricane, however, and it was the Hurricane that shot down more German aircraft in the battle than all the other British types put together.

During the Battle of Britain, the Observer Corps had six main types of German aircraft to identify and monitor. These were the Messerschmitt Bf109E, the Messerschmitt Bf110, the Junkers Ju87B, the Heinkel He111, the Dornier Do17Z and the Junkers Ju88A. Undoubtedly the most famous – and perhaps romantic – of these aircraft was the Messerschmitt Bf109E. The image that most people have of the battle is of the rival fighter aircraft engaged in mortal combat in the skies above southern England. The RAF's Hurricanes and Spitfires pitted against the Messerschmitt 109s of the Luftwaffe, like aerial war-horses, and piloted by latter-day knights in armour in a tournament of epic proportions. The main purpose of the German offensive was to bomb as many of Britain's resources as possible, the resulting destruction being intended to reduce the country's capacity to defend itself against the planned seaborne invasion. The bombers were, therefore, the Luftwaffe's main weapons, while the fighter aircraft, in the main, were used as escorts to protect the bomber formations against attack. The Messerschmitt Bf109E was considered to be as good a fighter in many respects as either the Spitfire or the Hurricane. Its two cannon fired explosive shells that could cause far more damage than the British fighters' Browning machine-guns, and its fuel-injected engine, compared with the carburettor-equipped Merlins, in some circumstances provided a more instant response. However, during much of the offensive it found itself extremely restricted because it had to remain close to the bomber formations, and its limited range meant that it couldn't remain over England for very long, without running short of fuel. Thus, for the Me109 to distract itself with too many personal engagements against the Royal Air Force would drain it of its life-blood.

The Messerschmitt Bf110 was a twin-engined two-seat aircraft. Its main task was to clear a path through Britain's defensive fighter screen, to allow the following bombers to pass through with the minimum of interference. But the Me110 fell an easy victim to the greater manoeuvrability of the English fighters, despite its fairly heavy armament; as a result it fared very badly in the battle and was lost in great numbers. The Luftwaffe had little alternative but to use the Me110 because of the shortage of 109s and also because of the latter's restricted range. As far as the Observer Corps was concerned, the Me110 had a far more distinctive shape than the Me109E; however, the single-engined fighter often had large sections painted in bright colours. This arrogant use of red or yellow made them instantly recognizable from quite a distance away.

The Junkers Ju87B, the famous Stuka, was another easily recognizable aircraft, primarily because of its gull-wing configuration and fixed undercarriage. It also made a very distinctive sound when attacking. As this two-seat dive-bomber hurtled towards its target its wind-driven siren would emit an ear-piercing and terrifying wailing sound, rising as the speed in the dive increased. The Ju87 was superb for its purpose of precision bombing, but when it encountered the British fighters it stood little chance of survival. Slow, poorly armed and unmanoeuvrable, it was, like the Me110, lost in great numbers and had to be withdrawn from the conflict. The Stuka had acquired a formidable reputation in Spain in 1936, reinforced in 1939 and 1940 in Poland, France and the Low Countries. The Germans had, however, ignored the fact that the dive-bomber's successes had been gained when the Luftwaffe had total air supremacy, as was not the case over Britain – the RAF's fighter pilots found the Stuka easy meat.

The three main aircraft used by the Germans for bombing were again very recognizable, and none more so than the Dornier Do17Z. As its nickname – 'Flying Pencil' – might suggest, this was a very sleek and elegant aircraft. Although the Dornier gained the tag at an earlier date and had been modified greatly by the time of the Battle of Britain, it still presented a long, slim profile in the sky. In fact, there was very little chance of the Observer Corps mistaking any of the German bombers. But the fact remained, of course, that, even at this busy time, the Observer Corps had to identify and monitor every aircraft in the sky, friend as well as foe.

The Royal Air Force deployed four main aircraft types in the battle: the Hawker Hurricane, the Boulton & Paul Defiant, the Bristol Blenheim and of course, probably the most easily recognizable British aircraft in those months, the Supermarine Spitfire. The Blenheim was a twin-engined high-speed light bomber, but its shape was so different from any of the German aircraft that it would have caused few recognition problems. The Heinkel He111, Dornier Do17 and Junkers Ju88 were all basically rounded at the nose, where extensive use was made of glass in order to improve vision for the bomb-aiming and machine-gun positions there. The nose of the Blenheim was altogether squarer and more wedge-like. The aircraft was often used at night when observation and tracking were more difficult, and many were later adapted to use airborne intercept radar. This was a new concept in early warning systems which proved highly successful, and the Blenheim IF came to be the backbone of RAF Fighter Command's night interception force. (The Germans made the same modification to the ill-starred Me110, with equal or even greater success.) Being a very light, high-speed bomber the Blenheim was also easily adapted to a fighter role. The Boulton & Paul Defiant when used as a day-fighter, as already discussed, proved a disaster in the battle, although it was later to restore its reputation somewhat when used as a night-fighter. The main damage to the Luftwaffe was caused by the Hurricanes and Spitfires, although another important factor in the victory, one which should never be overlooked, was the performance of the pilots themselves. Many experts maintain that although the Spitfire, particularly, and Messerschmitt 109 were very evenly matched, and proved worthy adversaries in many ways, it was the skill and courage of the British pilots that just gave them the edge. It must be said also that the Me109's limited 'time over target', and its need to stay with the bombers, severely hampered the German pilots.

If an invasion had been attempted (which depended in turn on the Luftwaffe succeeding in destroying the RAF and also gaining air supremacy), the Observer Corps would have played an active part in the defence of Britain. Home Defence staff officers would have been stationed at each Observer Corps centre, where the tracks of attacking airborne forces would have been displayed, thus enabling the small defending force available in this country to be used to best advantage.

During the Battle of Britain the Luftwaffe lost more than 1,400 aircraft between 10 July and the end of September 1940. They also lost many of their most experienced pilots and aircrew. The German casualties in men and aircraft effectively ended Hitler's invasion plans – the Third Reich was unable to sustain such catastrophic losses. More importantly, Britain had shown the world that Germany was by no means invincible.

Perhaps one of the most famous British fighter pilots, if not *the* most famous pilot, of the war, Squadron Leader Douglas Bader, flew with 242 (Hurricane) Squadron, based at Duxford, during the Battle of Britain. Late in the morning of Thursday, 11 July 1940, he was to make his first kill of the battle. It was a rainy day, so visibility was poor when he took off to investigate reports of an unidentified aircraft. Finding the intruder, he discovered it to be a Dornier 17. He therefore engaged it, only to see it disappear beneath the clouds. Bader was, however, confident that he had killed it, and five minutes after he had landed back at base the Observer Corps reported that they had seen the Dornier crash into the sea. The corps was increasingly to play an important part in the confirming or otherwise of 'kills', as well as in reporting the whereabouts of downed British aircraft and pilots.

The Observer Corps' busiest day during the battle, in terms of the number of enemy aircraft they had to plot, was 15 August; indeed, it was one of the most important days of the entire battle. To the Luftwaffe, which lost seventy-five aircraft, compared to the thirty-four of the Royal Air Force, it became known as 'Black Thursday', although they had proudly christened it beforehand *'Adlertag'* – 'Eagle Day'. Perhaps the most influential day, however, was exactly a month later, 15 September. For a few days it had been relatively quiet, and it remained so on the 15th until approximately 11am, when the first contacts appeared on the radar screen. More and more contacts were reported and it became clear that this was going to be no ordinary day. As fate would have it, Winston Churchill and his wife were spending the day at the Uxbridge operations room, which he likened to a small theatre with stalls and a circle: 'We took our seats in the dress circle. Below us was the large-scale map table, around which perhaps twenty highly trained young men and women, with their telephone assistants, assembled.' On this day (later to be officially designated as 'Battle of Britain Day') large formations of German bombers massed across the Channel, accompanied by every available fighter. The RDF had these formations tracked even before they left the coast of the Continent, and the RAF pilots, outnumbered and tired though they were, slew the wicked giant, like David killing Goliath. By the end of the day Germany could no longer mount a successful air offensive and the invasion had to be postponed.

In August 1940 Air Commodore Warrington-Morris had announced the institution of an Observer Corps fund to purchase a Supermarine Spitfire at a cost of £5,000. During the Diamond Jubilee celebrations of the Royal Observer Corps in 1985, approval was given for the markings on the Battle of Britain Memorial Flight Spitfire Mk IIa, P7350, to be changed. The aircraft was repainted to represent EB-Z of 41 Squadron, the aircraft donated to the Royal Air Force in 1940 by the Observer Corps, and displayed the embellishments of the original aircraft, P7666, which was the first Spitfire in the war to bear the legend 'Observer Corps.' It was issued to 41 Squadron at Hornchurch in November 1940. During its time there it was flown by Squadron Leader D. O. Finlay, DFC, and had an eventful career. On its very first sortie it shot down a Messerschmitt Bf109. Even though EB-Z suffered considerable damage in that engagement, it was soon in action again above Dover, where on its second sortie it destroyed yet another Me109. On its third and final mission for 41 Squadron, Finlay participated in the destruction of one more 109, before, in February 1941, EB-Z was transferred to 54 Squadron, also based at Hornchurch, and re-lettered as KL-Z.

By 1941 the Battle of Britain was well and truly over. Now, instead of keeping all its aeroplanes at the ready to repel the onslaughts of the Luftwaffe, the RAF could actually send aircraft back across the Channel, to patrol the skies above France. KL-Z was taking part in one of these patrols when it came under attack from an Me109. In the dogfight which ensued, the pilot of the Observer Corps Spitfire dived from 20,000 feet with the Messerchmitt in hot pursuit. The Spitfire pulled out at zero feet, causing his attacker to plunge straight into the sea. The very brief, but nevertheless successful history of P7666 ended on 20 April 1941, when it was shot down by Me109s.

P7350, the Battle of Britain Flight Spitfire, had quite a history

Squadron Leader D.O. Finlay standing in front of Spitfire II P7666, the first aircraft donated by the OC in 1941. (© Crown copyright 1993/MOD reproduced with permission of the Controller of HMSO)

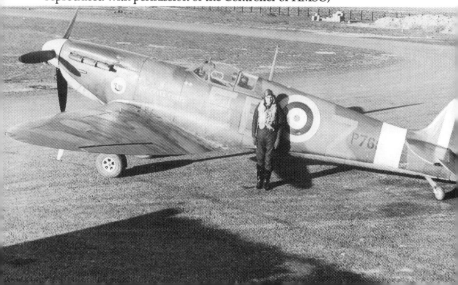

itself. Built at the Castle Bromwich aircraft factory in Birmingham in 1940, she was only the fourteenth out of the 11,989 Spitfires built there, and arrived at RAF Brize Norton on 17 August 1940. From September 1940 she served with 266 (Rhodesia) Squadron at RAF Wittering. During the rest of the war she also saw service with 603 (City of Edinburgh) Squadron, Auxiliary Air Force; 616 (County of South Yorkshire) Squadron, AAF; 64 Squadron; the Central Gunnery School at RAF Sutton Bridge; and No 57 Operational Training Unit. During the war she shot down three enemy aircraft, and in July 1944 she was put into storage with No 39 Maintenance Unit at RAF Colerne. In 1967, after twenty-four years on the ground, she was loaned to Spitfire Productions Limited for use in the film *Battle of Britain*, and was again painted in her Battle of Britain colours. After being made airworthy again she flew from Henlow to Duxford in May 1968, her first flight in all those twenty-four years. After the film was completed (it was released in 1969), the aircraft was presented to the Battle of Britain Memorial Flight.

Post crew at Great Bedwyn 1941. Rear from left to right: N. Tilley, L/Obs G. Kempster, T. Alexander, G. Bushnel, F.S. Turgess, S. Bolland, P. Hoare, H. Picken. Front: A. Shefford, J. Bowyer, W. Lovelock, C/Obs J. Lloyd, T. Cummings, G. Gauler, A. Standing. (ROCM/Jack Barter).

Air Vice-Marshal J.E. (Johnnie) Johnson
CB CBE DSO DFC DL

During the Battle of Britain our radars saw gaggles of enemy bombers and fighters assembling over the Pas de Calais, after they had formed-up, setting course for their targets in Southern England. Sometimes these great enemy formations were ten, or more, miles long and Air Vice-Marshal Keith Park who fought the battle from his 11 Group headquarters, wanted to know exactly where and when the vanguard crossed our coast so that he could scramble his fighters. This vital information was provided by the Corps' watchers.

Sometimes during those monumentous days small enemy raids slipped in unseen by our radars and again the watchers provided vital information about the aggressor's height and direction as they did, also, when low-level raids came in below our radar coverage.

The Royal Observer Corps was an integral part of our defence organisation and played a vital part in the waging and winning of the Battle of Britain.

Johnnie Johnson.

IN THE HOUR OF PERIL
OFFICERS AND MEN OF THE
ROYAL OBSERVER CORPS
EARNED THE GRATITUDE
OF THE BRITISH NATIONS
SUSTAINING THE VALOUR OF
THE ROYAL AIR FORCE
AND FORTIFYING THE CAUSE
OF FREEDOM
BY THE GIFT OF
SPITFIRE AIRCRAFT
They shall mount up with wings as eagles.
Issued by the Ministry of Aircraft Production 1941

Above left: Air Vice-Marshal J.E. (Johnnie) Johnson. (AVM J.E. Johnson)
Above right: Presentation plaque from Ministry of Aircraft Production for ROC Spitfire. (ROCM/Jack Barter) **Below:** Winter scene at Dorchester post during the Second World War. (ROCM/Henry Wills)

The real success won by the air and ground forces in the Battle of Britain can be attributed to a lot of factors, but at the end of the day the part played by Dowding should not be underestimated. Until the end of May 1940, while the Battle for France still raged, Britain was committed to sending more and more of its fighter aircraft across the Channel to support its ally. It was due to the efforts of Dowding, and in the teeth of opposition from Churchill, that sufficient aircraft remained on British soil to face the Germans after France had fallen. If the government had continued to send fighters to the Continent, things might have been very different. To the French, the battle being fought on their soil was the decisive one. From the British point of view, however, the Battle of Britain would be the decisive conflict, since to lose it would be to lose everything. To win it, on the other hand, would mean that the war would go on and the British Isles could remain the springboard for any future attacks against the Third Reich. Of the Observer Corps, Air Chief Marshal Sir Hugh Dowding stated in his dispatch on the battle:

It is important to note that at this time the Observer Corps constituted the whole means of tracking enemy raids once they had crossed the coastline ... Their task throughout was quite invaluable. Without it the air-raid warning systems could not have been operated and inland interceptions would rarely have been made.

Air Vice-Marshal Johnnie Johnson suggests (in his *History of Air Fighting*) that it was a near-run battle even so. The Luftwaffe could have won air domination over southern England within two weeks had they set about attacking the right targets. General Kreipe of the Luftwaffe considered that Germany's defeat at the hands of the RAF ultimately lost them the war. Air Vice-Marshal Park suggested that faulty German tactics were a major factor in ensuring their defeat, while Johnson noted that the targets they should have aimed for in those first few days were radars, sector stations and headquarters, and the coastal airfields. And it is my opinion that the Observer Corps posts could easily have been added to that list. In 1940 Sir Archibald Sinclair, the Air Minister, conveyed a message to the corps, which makes a fitting dedication to all those men and women who gave up so much of their time in their country's defence. 'By your vigilance and faithful devotion to duty you are making an indispensable contribution to the achievements of our fighter pilots. Their victories are your victories too.'

The defence of this country during the Battle of Britain, although often pictured as a perfect machine, did have its shortcomings. I hope that in this chapter I have shown some of these defects, without in any way belittling the wonderful achievement of the men and women who took part. The fact remains that during Britain's darkest hour in modern times, the enthusiasm and courage of the nation pulled through to victory. A tribute to the part played by the Observer Corps, and all the other ground services I have described, is a tribute to the British public.

CHAPTER FOUR
Reorganization of the Royal Observer Corps

Even though the war wheels were still in motion in 1941, the Observer Corps now had a small breathing-space that had been denied them in 1940. This respite meant that improvements to the system of organization and operation could be considered. For the corps, the first major event of the year was the announcement that it would be granted the prefix 'Royal', and from 9 April 1941 it was officially renamed the Royal Observer Corps.

In a broadcast made by Air Commodore R. V. Goddard in 1941, the Observer Corps' contribution to the air battle was again praised.

Of all our air defences, I think the searchlight and balloon crews and the Observer Corps have about the most thankless tasks. No one knows how much is owed to the balloon and searchlight men for the moral effect they exert on the enemy. We do know occasionally, when bits of aeroplane get washed ashore with cable wire twisted round them, that some balloon crew has earned a good night's sleep. We know, too, but less tangibly, the fending-off effect of our searchlights as well as their power to reveal the black Boche when he comes low enough. But do we all realise that the Observer Corps has been the foundation of our Fighter Defence? That Corps of veteran volunteers must have taken a quiet pride in their vital but little known part in the Battle of Britain.

In the March-May 1941 issue of *Hutchinson's Pictorial History of the War*, the Observer Corps was again praised, in an article entitled, 'The Battle of Britain, how the Royal Air Force shattered the Nazi Luftwaffe in their attempt to gain mastery of the air'.

The task of the controller in setting the stage for the battle is governed by one factor, accurate and timely information about the raids. In clear weather with little or no cloud, the raiders came over at such high altitude that they were almost invisible even with the use of binoculars. The numbers of aircraft employed made a confusion of noise in the high atmosphere and thus increased the difficulty of detecting raids by sound. In cloudy weather this difficulty was increased for the Observer Corps had then to rely entirely on sound. In view of these difficulties, that Corps and other sources of information deserve very great credit for the remarkably clear and timely picture of the situation they presented to the controllers.

The attacks on London on 7th September were made in two or three distinct waves at intervals of about twenty minutes, the whole attack lasting up to an hour. The waves were composed of formations of from twenty to forty bombers with an equal number of fighters in close escort, additional protection being given by large formations of other fighters flying at a much higher altitude. Most of the German aircraft came over at heights above fifteen thousand feet in sunny skies which made the task of the Observer Corps very difficult.

The problem remained that the identification of aircraft by sound alone was nearly impossible. As Air Marshal Philip Joubert de la Ferté was to admit in a broadcast:

Our best scientists worked for two years in an attempt to analyse the sound made by various aeroplanes, and thus to enable our ground defences to get over one of their greatest difficulties, the identification of hostile aircraft at night or in cloud. At the end of the two years they had to confess themselves defeated. [Perhaps these scientists were the same crackpots who thought up the 'Death Ray' idea.] The other night I was trying to sleep while a constant stream of what I supposed were German bombers passed overhead. I identified them in the same way as most people do, by the deep, uneven droning note of the engines. About four o'clock in the morning I was awakened by a different sound, much more even and higher pitched, which I thought belonged to one of our twin-engined night bombers. I hopped out of bed and looked out, only to be greeted by six very loud bangs from the bombs of the aircraft which I had supposed to be friendly. So I still say that I cannot guarantee to distinguish friend from foe by the sound, although here in London one can make a pretty good guess.

Often the problem with locating high-flying aircraft at night by sound was to pin-point their actual location. Assuming a raider passes overhead at 25,000 feet and is flying at 300 mph, the sound of its engine will not in fact be heard on the ground until it has passed nearly two miles beyond the overhead point. For the Observer Corps this was just a matter of statistics, but for the anti-aircraft gunners it proved a major problem. To hit the raider in this example, the AA gunner would have to aim at a point four miles farther still. Then, provided the raider did not alter course, speed or height – as they almost invariably did when under fire – the bomber and shell would theoretically meet. Even by day and firing at a visible target, the AA gunner spotting a high-flying raider would still have to allow for the several miles it would have travelled before the shell reached it. For example, an aircraft sighted over Middlesbrough might not be shot down until it reached Stockton, four miles away.

One of the most famous tracks that the Royal Observer Corps made during the war was undoubtedly that of Rudolf Hess. When, on 10 May 1941, Hess, the Deputy Fuehrer and friend, secretary and confidant of Hitler, flew himself to Scotland in a Messerschmitt Bf110, observers of No 30 (later No 23) Group, Durham, 31 Group, Galashiels, and 34 Group, Glasgow, tracked the aircraft from the moment it flew across the Northumberland coast until its eventual crash in Scotland on the edge of Eaglesham Moor. Both the crash and the parachute descent were observed in bright moonlight by the members of H2 Post.

Due to the increased call-up of manpower during the war, women were first recruited into the corps in September 1941. It seems odd, now, that the corps took so long to employ female observers, since all the other branches of Fighter Command's network of defences had employed women from the start of the war. Radar observers, for instance, were recruited almost exclusively from the Womens' Auxiliary Air Force (WAAF), and became highly skilled at estimating target bearings, heights, ranges, and aircraft numbers. Also, pictorial and film evidence would suggest that the majority of staff employed in the ops rooms at Fighter Command group headquarters were women, affectionately known as 'the beauty chorus'. It may be that the job of observer was considered unsuitable for women, as it entailed spending many hours in the open. Life on a post was very uncomfortable and observers were likely to get extremely wet and cold; sometimes, during the Battle of Britain, they were even fired upon. The first women observers were used mainly as tellers and plotters at the area centres, a job which had similarities to the work done by the beauty chorus at Fighter Command group HQs. However, a great many women showed a keen interest in working at the posts themselves. In addition, many had chosen to join the Royal Observer Corps in preference to nursing, the Land Army, or factory work. Advertisements urged women to 'do a front-line job and live at home', and newspaper articles praised the attractive uniform and excellent working conditions. But, as already explained, conditions were in fact less than glamorous, especially on the posts. They were also the same for the women as they were for the men, the only restriction being a moral one – it was considered improper for a woman to work the night shift with a man. By early 1944 centre crews were predominantly female, and several Observer Corps Groups had all-female crews. It would appear, however, that the very first women to join the organization were met with extreme suspicion and trepidation. It was soon recognized, however, that the feminine and rather delicate appearance of these new recruits was extremely misleading. They were swiftly to prove their resilience; indeed, some centres even allowed them to work round the clock. With this new supply of young, fresh and alert minds, the decision was made to retire centre crews at fifty, the idea being to replace the older men with young women. As the organization had always been a male domain, with many of its members being 'older men,' this decision was not greeted with open arms. Questions were asked in Parliament. At the end of the

Above: Certificate of employment in the Royal Observer Corps belonging to Gwendoline May Easton dated 10 July 1944. (ROCM/Obs Off Norman Parker)
Below: Young ladies from Winchester Control meet American airmen during a visit to Greenham Common 8 July 1944. (ROCM/Stan Jewell)

day, however, the young women proved their worth, and increased efficiency into the bargain.

When the Air/Sea Rescue Service was introduced in 1941, the Royal Observer Corps, along with the police, the Mercantile Marine, the Coastguard Service, and the Royal National Lifeboat Institution, formed a very active part of this joint Air Ministry and Admiralty scheme. In 1941, another large-scale battle around Britain was still considered to be a possibility, and so a joint directorate of the Air Ministry and the Admiralty, known as the Directorate of Air/Sea Rescue Services, was set up. The director was Air Commodore L. G. Le B. Croke, and the deputy director was Captain C. L. Howe, RN. This organization co-ordinated a network of services for the rescue of airmen who came down in the sea, or the crews of stricken ships. Previously the work had been carried out by a part of the marine section of RAF Coastal Command, but the constant expansion of the Royal Air Force, with a consequent increase in the risk of bomber crews or fighter pilots being forced down into the sea, led to the creation of Air/Sea Rescue.

The Royal Observer Corps posts along the coastline would contact the local police station immediately they saw an aircraft or airman down in the sea, and the police would notify the nearest aerodrome, which in turn would send out aircraft carrying supplies. Rescue craft would also be launched, and would be in direct wireless communication with the aircraft, which would guide them to the spot. The RAF had its own launches. Sixty-three feet long and propelled by three Napier aero-engines, each of 500 horsepower, they had a top speed of 40 mph and a cruising speed of 32 mph. Air/Sea Rescue also used amphibian aircraft, one of which, the Supermarine Seagull V, a pusher biplane, had been designed by R. J. Mitchell, designer of the Spitfire. From 1941 many Allied airmen shot down at sea owed their lives to rescue flights by Supermarine Walruses, the RAF's version of the Seagull.

In June 1942 Air Commodore G. H. Ambler took over from Air Commodore Warrington-Morris as Commandant of the Royal Observer Corps. By this time, most observers had been issued with uniforms that were based on the standard RAF

Rt. Hon. Lord Callaghan of Cardiff KG

HOUSE OF LORDS

Those of us who were in or around London and
the Home Counties while the Battle of Britain
was being fought overhead, and the bombs were
falling, will never forget either the
gallantry of the young men of the Royal Air
Force or the steadfastness and dedication of
those who served on the ground in the Royal
Observer Corps. The members of the Corps were
right in the front line as they searched the
skies for enemy aircraft; they played their
part in rescuing the airmen who had been shot
down and, much later, played an important role
both when the doodle-bugs were directed
against us, and in the Normandy landings.

I suppose, like the rest of us, the Royal
Observer Corps had to fade away, but I am
delighted that memories of its work will be
kept alive by this history and tribute.

James Callaghan

Above: Observer Corps post at Harrow during the early stages of the Second World War. (ROCM/Mrs S. Fulcher) **Inset:** The Rt. Hon. Lord Callaghan of Cardiff KG. (Lord Callaghan)

battledress, with a cloth corps badge on the left breast of the uniform blouse. Air Commodore Ambler proposed and indeed activated a number of changes within the organization, of which the main modifications fell into six categories: 1) reorganization of Royal Observer Corps headquarters; 2) reorganization of area headquarters; 3) area territory to conform with the appropriate fighter groups; 4) greater employment of young women at centres; 5) training to become compulsory and to be the official responsibility of Headquarters, Royal Observer Corps; 6) reorganization of the corps on a non-military basis, but with graded ranks.

The first of Ambler's reorganizations to take effect was the adjustment of each area to conform with that of the fighter group with which it was concerned. These changes didn't effect the Southern and Western Areas, because they already corresponded approximately with the areas covered, respectively, by Nos 11 and 10 Fighter Command Groups. Having altered the area territories it was then decided that the best plan was to move the Royal Observer Corps area headquarters to locations closer to their respective fighter group HQs. There were now six of these: Scottish, Northern,

Crew C at Yeovil Centre in March 1943. Rear from left to right: F. Phippen, L. Rendall, A. Chapman, H. Priddy, C. Quarrell, W. Goodland, S. Hyde, L. Pike, J. MacGarry, K. Selwood. Centre: A. Pearcy, J. Ewing, A. Lucas, H. Bulson, T. Abbott, F. Ewens, J. Mills, S. Sibley, N. Snell, E. Wakely, R. Vincent. Front: M. Dyson, M. Grant, M. Jones, W. Snell, J. Spinner, A. Sage, K. Snell, M. Mead, F. Hyde. (ROCM/Barbara Freke)

North-Western, Midland, Southern and Western. However, the RAF decided to close down Fighter Command No 13 Group, which meant that the corps' Northern Area ceased to exist. The groups and all the observation posts that had been within Northern Area were reallocated to either Scottish Area or Midland Area. As a result, the Royal Observer Corps now had only five remaining areas.

Until this time a centre controller had been responsible for the running and administration of each Observer Corps operations room, the posts that supplied the ops rooms with information being looked after by observer group officers. It was decided to appoint a group commandant to unify the policy within each group. The group commandant would be assisted by a deputy group commandant (DGC), and an adjutant was appointed to handle the administration within the group. Duty controllers were appointed at the rank of observer officer to take charge of each crew at the operations rooms, and observer officers were also appointed to look after the administration and smooth running of the posts. A post observer officer would cover quite a large area and have a number of posts to administer. Training of observers had varied between the groups, but there was no established training method. Group headquarters therefore undertook the responsibility for training; methods were standardised and a full programme was instituted in each of the groups.

At every post throughout the country, one observer was appointed as a training instructor, with the rank of leading observer. The observer who had traditionally been in charge of the post, known as the head observer, was now given the title chief observer, and became responsible to his group officer for the administration of the post. The leading observer acted as deputy to the chief observer. Group officers were made to attend compulsory training courses so that they, in turn, could instruct the leading observers in the most up-to-date training methods. The previous system of using A and B members was still employed because there was a need for part-time as well as full-time observers. The Class A members had to be over thirty-five years of age and did fifty-six hours of duty each .

week, while Class B members, who were mainly young people and those in reserved occupations, had to do up to twenty-four hours' duty a week, which made it quite a busy part-time schedule. A new system was now set up whereby each post had to hold a weekly training meeting. There were also periodic training visits of post personnel to the operations rooms. Finally, a periodic test became compulsory for all post observers.

As well as duty controllers being promoted to the rank of observer officer, their was a further rank structure for personnel at the operations room. The duty controller's assistant took the rank of chief observer, as did the post controller, while the floor supervisor was appointed to the rank of leading observer.

The Royal Observer Corps had always been represented at the Fighter Command group headquarters operations room by the liaison officer, who was now, under the reorganization, given the rank of observer lieutenant. The liaison service was actually extended by providing representation in the sector operations rooms, where the corps representative held the rank of chief observer and was known as a sector liaison teller.

All ranks in the Royal Observer Corps related to equivalent ranks in the Royal Air Force. An observer – the basic rank for post and operations room personnel – was equivalent to an aircraftman; leading observer to a corporal; chief observer to a sergeant; observer officer to a flying officer; observer lieutenant to a flight lieutenant; observer lieutenant-commander to a squadron leader; observer commander to a wing commander; and observer captain to a group captain. Each of the five areas had an area commandant holding the rank of observer captain, while the deputy area commandant and the group commandants held the rank of observer commander and the deputy group commandant held the rank of observer lieutenant-commander. The rank of the Commandant depended on whether he had been a serving RAF officer, in which case he would be an air commodore, but if he had been a senior Royal Observer Corps full-time officer he would, on appointment, take the rank of observer commodore.

Air Commodore Ambler had proved to be a great influence

on the corps, bringing the organization forward in leaps and bounds. His main achievement was to change completely the image of the corps from that of a group of odd eccentrics who huddled up in duffle-coats to watch aeroplanes through binoculars, to that of a smart, well-organized, semi-military organization with a much closer association with the Royal Air Force. While his reforms were still taking place, however, Ambler returned to Fighter Command and was succeeded by Air Commodore Finlay Crerar, who remained as Commandant until November 1945.

Even though the Battle of Britain was over, and the Royal Observer Corps, like other units of the ground defence system, had occasion to review its efficiency, the war against British cities was to continue with venom. The price of the RAF's success in the Battle of Britain was the nightly bombardment of cities and towns, as Roy Conyers Nesbit pointed out in *An Illustrated History of the RAF*:

However, Fighter Command, by then commanded by Air Marshal Sir W. Sholto Douglas, did not at this time possess any specialized night-fighters, but depended instead on Blenheims and obsolescent Defiants. The air-interception radar fitted to the Blenheims had a limited range, while the aircraft was slower than many of the attacking bombers. Hurricane and Spitfire squadrons were pressed into service but the usual method of attack was visual, often carried out in the middle of anti-aircraft fire and searchlights. Ground control of night fighters was inadequate, partly because the Chain Home radar system was directed only towards the sea. Inland tracking depended on the Royal Observer Corps who, although extremely accurate during the day, experienced more difficulties at night.

During the early Blitz on London, the balloon barrage usually flew at about 5,000 feet, and the searchlights were largely ineffective above 12,000 feet; there was also the problem of anti-aircraft fire not being able to reach the higher altitudes. But slowly Britain began once again to gain the upper hand, despite the dreadful loss of life among civilians. The barrage and anti-aircraft defences around London were tremendously ' strengthened, and the tide was further turned with the invention of the Mark IV air-interception radar, which was fitted to the cannon-armed Beaufighter. Suddenly, the course of the battle began to turn and the Luftwaffe began to suffer heavy losses of its bombers.

Germany adopted a new tactic of sending hit-and-run raiders against the south and south-east coasts of England, in a bid to destroy shipping and thus the potential to launch an invasion against the French mainland. The German pilots had learned that when they flew low the British radar system was not always able to detect them. It was decided that the Royal Observer Corps could be employed as a means of combating these raids, and so a large number of what were termed satellite posts were constructed, very quickly, all along the coast. These satellite posts were able to give complete low-level coverage. The enemy aircraft were detected as soon as they reached the coastline and, through an adapted communications network, RAF fighters were soon airborne, forcing the raiders to turn back, or shooting them down into the Channel. Air-raid warnings to several coastal towns were sounded directly from the Observer Corps posts.

On 23 January 1942, *The Aeroplane* published an article entitled 'Forewarmed is Forearmed. A Guide to the Royal Observer Corps'. Written by A. C. Trinder, it again provides a mixture of seriousness and fun, which seems to have been the manner in which most writers then approached the subject:

This little treatise, which we humbly dedicate to our O.G.O., is intended to heal a running sore upon the body politic: - namely, that nobody has ever heard of the Royal Observer Corps. Quite a lot of people have heard of the A.T.S., the A.F.S., the W.A.A.F.s and the G.F.S.; they make frequent visits to G. & S. and large numbers of them belong to the R.A.C. But do they know what R.O.C. stands for? They do not. And what would they do if they did know? We believe they would all join at once!

The R.O.C. is the eyes and ears of Fighter Command. The first plot known was a sound plot on an enemy patrol obtained in Rome in 390 B.C. by the Capitoline Geese. Had it not been for these watchful observers the City would have fallen, and there would have been no Mussolini. After this there is no further evidence of Observers' activities until the famous event depicted upon the badge issued to all Observers. This shows a member of a coastal post of the Royal Elizabethan Observer Corps obtaining a visual on the Spanish Armada in the glorious year 1588. Here again the country was saved, otherwise there would have been no Winston Churchill. Being aware that comfort spells efficiency, Queen Elizabeth decreed that all Posts should be provided with a blazing bonfire (which can be seen on the badge) to keep the Observers warm. This is the origin of the Corps' motto - 'Forewarmed is Forearmed'.

After this the Corps appears to have been disbanded. The mere threat of its revival was enough to deter a projected invasion by Napoleon, though it is true that another Frenchman, Louis Blériot, succeeded in landing completely unchallenged in 1909.

But on the outbreak of war with Germany in 1939 the Corps immediately sprang into prominence. All posts were continuously manned and each member eagerly began to scan the heavens for Göring's Vaunted Luftwaffe. The extreme difficulty of their task in these early days can only be appreciated when it is realised that the sole German Aircraft seen over the country previously had been the *Graf Zeppelin*.

Wartime observer studying silhouettes of enemy and allied aircraft from large identification sheets that were put on the wall of the observation hut. (Virtue & Co Ltd)

CHAPTER FIVE
D-Day and the Seaborne Observers

'Operation Overlord' was the name given to the Allied invasion of Europe, which began with D-Day on 6 June 1944. For some time before the invasion, the Commander-in-Chief of the Allied air forces, Air Chief Marshal Leigh-Mallory, expressed concern about the increasing numbers of aircraft that were being shot down by friendly fire. Leigh-Mallory, in discussion with Air Commodore Crerar, the Commandant of the Royal Observer Corps, decided that there was a need for observers trained in aircraft recognition to advise gun crews on board the 'defensively equipped merchant ships' (DEMS) during the invasion. The scheme, which became known as 'Seaborne', initially provided for naval gunners to be trained in aircraft recognition, but the Air Chief Marshal himself suggested that Royal Observer Corps personnel should be used. The idea was at first rejected by the Air Ministry, but as the losses of Allied planes to friendly fire increased, the situation became critical.

The Central School of Aircraft Recognition had been established to teach instructors within the Allied air forces. Its intended students were drawn from the RAF, the Royal Canadian Air Force, the Royal Australian Air Force, the Royal New Zealand Air Force, the RAF Regiment, the United States Eighth and Ninth Air Forces, and the Royal Observer Corps. The methods adopted by the school were broadly similar to the earlier aircraft recognition courses, and employed large scale models and wall-charts showing the silhouettes of aircraft in various attitudes. As a result, the RAF and the Army anti-aircraft crews already had experts in aircraft recognition, but as plans for the invasion got under way in earnest, it was obvious that these men were going to be very busy carrying out the jobs for which they had already been trained. So, after much reconsideration, Leigh-Mallory's plan was adopted. The Royal Observer Corps was to play yet another supporting role in the

Seaborne Observers at the DEMS Depot, Royal Bath Hotel Bournemouth in 1944. Rear from left to right: R. Wilson, J. Pendleton, E. Gibson, J. Steele. Front: Derek Tasker, George Coward, Dougie Harmsworth, L.G. Davies. (ROCM/John Ledge)

great events about to take place.

After the decision had been made, a letter was sent from the Commandant to all posts and centres. Dated 28 April 1944, it read as follows:

Confidential. A personal message from the Commandant of the Corps to every member. 1. I write this message to each of you in every Post in the Kingdom and I want you to read it very carefully; I want each of you to consider carefully your own position and make up your mind which path yours must be at this most important crossroads. Much depends on your decision. 2. Many of you have asked me from time to time whether you could have the chance of taking part in more active operations and I believe many of you who have for so long been on the defensive, will welcome the chance to join in the offensive. I can tell you now of what is not only the most important operational requirement but a handsome and well-deserved tribute to the skill and value of the Corps to the Fighting Services. 3. The Supreme Command has asked me to provide a considerable number of ROC observers to serve on board ship for recognition duties during the forthcoming operations. The highest importance is attached to this request, for inefficient and faulty recognition has contributed largely to enemy success against our shipping and to our losses of aircraft from friendly fire. This request is one which demands the best which the Corps can give; it calls for skill in instant recognition, readiness to share the hardships of the Fighting Services in amphibious operations and personal sacrifice on behalf of those members left behind who must carry on. 4. For a long time now the Corps has been confined to a place on the Home Front - an essential and important place, but still a long way from the real offensive. Many of us who knew its skill and value to the Air Force have wished it could go with them overseas but have had to be content at home. The chance has come. It is a great opportunity and I consider it to be one of the most important events in the history of the Corps, a long and honourable history. We must not let this opportunity pass. No other organization possess our skill and experience in aircraft recognition. Our invasion forces need something which we have got. 5. Read the special Air Ministry Order which gives all the details of the scheme which has been worked out. You will see that when you volunteer for a month's (or preferably two months') service, you will have entered into the Royal Navy. Every effort will be made to arrange for any two Observers so wishing to serve together in the same ship. 6. Notice also that you will wear ROC uniform with a Naval armband; and particularly that you will wear a shoulder flash SEABORNE. I hope and believe that this flash will create history in the ROC and build up for itself and the Corps a prestige in the public eye. Authority will be sought for it to continue to be worn by Observers after return to the Corps from special duty. If that is given I am sure it will be a much coveted distinction. 7. I have said that this demand will mean strenuous effort and sacrifice on the part of those left behind. While this scheme is of the highest importance, the primary role of the Corps must not be endangered. The Air Defence of Great Britain will have as great responsibilities as ever. Those who volunteer for Seaborne Service will be accepting active service hazards; those who remain behind will have to fill their places. I am confident that you will cheerfully play your part whatever it entails and that the reputation of the Royal Observer Corps will shine more brightly than ever.

In all, 1,326 observers, including twenty officers, responded to the Commandant's letter. A depot had been set up at Bournemouth for selection and training, and was capable of handling 150 observers a week. Each observer had to take a trade test, of which 209 failed to qualify, and a further eighty-one failed the medical. Some of those who were rejected volunteered to transfer to posts on the south coast, thus releasing other observers for seaborne duty. Those observers that passed the initial stages were formed into squadrons, each consisting of two flights of fifteen men. What followed was a week of intensive training, which not only involved aircraft recognition, but also had to make sailors out of the land-loving observers in a very short time. The Royal Navy gave a series of lectures about arcane things called dhobying, ditty-boxes and bum-boats. The observers also learned about the defence systems on board the ships that they were training to advise, such as Oerlikon guns and PAC rockets.

As each course was completed, the seaborne observers, now, with the rank of petty officer, were quickly detached to their respective ships, most of which were at Southampton or Portsmouth; about half of them went to American vessels. The ships were often assault landing ships, the parent vessels to the small assault craft, and were manned by the Merchant Navy, DEMS ratings, Royal Marines and Maritime Royal Artillery, who crewed the guns. The observers, like almost everyone on board, now faced a monotonous wait, which was temporarily allayed when King George VI reviewed the fleet.

Six and a half thousand ships took part in the invasion. The first of these into the beaches carried the assault troops, but they had to be backed up by a continuous stream of support vessels carrying supplies and reinforcements. The convoys operated beneath an 'umbrella' of Allied fighters such as Mustangs, Thunderbolts, Lightnings, Typhoons and Spitfires, all displaying the black-and-white invasion stripes on wings and tail, an extra aid to recognition.

The invasion took the form of a five-pronged assault along a 50-mile stretch of the Normandy coastline between Cherbourg and the River Orne. The beaches on which the American, British and Canadian forces landed were code-named 'Utah', 'Omaha', 'Gold', 'Juno' and 'Sword'.

The following account is from Ivor Matanle's *World War II:*

Going ashore on D-Day from the sea were 57,500 American and over 75,000 British and Canadian troops, plus 900 armoured vehicles and 600 guns. A remarkable total of 13,743 aircraft took part, including those that landed the 27,000 airborne troops on the night of June 5th/6th by parachute and in the force of 867 towed gliders. The first attack was to be by these three airborne divisions, landing from midnight onwards just inland from the coast to the west of the main landing area, and securing vital bridges and positions prior to the amphibious assault. From 6.30 am onwards, the landings were scheduled for five major beaches - the US 1st Army on Utah and Omaha Beaches, west and east of the Vire estuary; the British 2nd Army on Gold Beach at Arromanches, and on Sword Beach between Lion-sur-Mer and Ouistreham; and the Canadians, also part of the British 2nd Army, on Juno Beach between Bernières and St Aubin. As June 5th, the scheduled day for the invasion, approached, the weather began to look worse by the hour. On June 4th, confident that not even the British would be mad enough to launch themselves upon their greatest adventure in gales and torrential rain, Rommel left France and went to visit his family in Ulm. On the next day, the fleet was actually at sea in appalling conditions when it was ordered back. Finally, despite continuing bad weather, Eisenhower, quite literally, decided to chance going ahead. So much organisational and logistic effort had gone into getting the fleet to sea that to delay longer meant an almost greater risk than launching the invasion in unfavourable conditions. D-Day was on.

As it turned out, the Luftwaffe hardly used its own air strength during the invasion, except for tip-and-run raids at night, laying mines and haphazard bombing. The Germans, convinced at first that this was not the main invasion, kept many forces, including Luftwaffe squadrons, in reserve, and the Allies achieved complete air superiority. A seaborne observer might have seen about three hostile aircraft if he was lucky, and so had little opportunity of using his skills against the enemy. They were, however, still able to perform their original task of restraining gun crews from opening fire on Allied aircraft, huge numbers of which were engaged in carpet-bombing the enemy positions just ahead of the advancing troops.

Royal Observer Corps casualties during the invasion and in the following support campaign included Percy Heading, who was on board the SS *Sambut* when it was sunk by shellfire; he received shrapnel wounds in his arms and legs. Chief Observer John B. Bancroft was killed by an acoustic mine exploding under the *Derry Cunily* on 24 June, and on 2 July Bill Slater was killed when the SS *Empire Broadsword* was sunk, again by mines.

Many observers made trips back and forth with the supply vessels from Britain to the beachheads, while others spent a dangerous month or more anchored off the French coast, waiting for their cargoes to be unloaded. But two and a half months after D-Day, the operation was officially over. The Bournemouth depot was closed down, and all the seaborne observers returned to duty at their posts ashore. For their service during the invasion ten observers were Mentioned in Dispatches: G. A. D. Bourne, J. D. Whitham, A. E. Llewellyn, G. McAllen, J. Hughes, T. H. Bodill, E. Jones, A. W. P. Dearden, D. N. James and J. W. Reynolds. All who took part received the France and Germany Star, as well as the 1939-1945 War Medal.

Air Chief-Marshal Leigh-Mallory was to have the final word on the scheme which had been his own brainchild. His letter to the Commandant of the Royal Observer Corps, circulated amongst all observers and officers, read:

I have read reports from both pilots and naval officers regarding the seaborne volunteers on board merchant ships during the recent operations. All reports agree that the seaborne volunteers have more than fulfilled their duties and have undoubtedly saved many of our aircraft from being engaged by ships' guns. I should be grateful if you would please convey to all ranks of the Royal Observer Corps, and in particular to the seaborne volunteers themselves, how grateful I, and all pilots in the Allied Expeditionary Air Force, are for their assistance, which has contributed in no small measure to the safety of our own aircraft, and also to the efficient protection of the ships at sea. The work of the Royal Observer Corps is often quite unjustly overlooked, and receives little recognition, and I therefore wish that the service they have rendered on this occasion be as widely advertised as possible, and all Units of the Air Defence of Great Britain are therefore to be informed of the success of this latest venture of the Royal Observer Corps.

CHAPTER SIX
Doodlebugs over Britain

No sooner was the invasion under way than Britain was subjected to a new terror. The Defence Committee had been aware for some time that Hitler's scientists had been developing new and awesome weapons of destruction; indeed, the committee was actually expecting this new phase of enemy air activity, which employed what became known as the 'flying- bomb'. There had been a great deal of concern and doubt about whether or not the Royal Observer Corps would be able to deal with a threat of this kind, not least because nobody knew the exact nature or capabilities of Germany's terror weapons. Doubters were soon proved wrong, however, as the Observer Corps rose to the challenge with a high degree of flexibility and alertness.

The very first flying-bombs over Britain were picked up on 13 June 1944, just a few days after D-Day, by observers in the coastal post at Dymchurch. The detection and subsequent reporting of the attack was so good that Churchill himself had been telephoned by Air Marshal Roderic Hill, C-in-C of 12 Group RAF, within three minutes of the first flying-bomb crossing the coast. Within seconds the defence system had been put into operation.

Unlike enemy aircraft, which could be engaged in battle, the flying-bombs steered a relentless and undeviating course. Their interception and destruction was therefore a matter of extreme urgency, and drastic measures would have to be taken to combat them. RAF controllers actually moved their equipment to the Royal Observer Corps operations rooms at Horsham and Maidstone, in order to be able to vector fighter aircraft directly from the information on the ROC plotting tables. The corps had a more immediate role to play in the crisis than it had ever known before, which inevitably gave observers at the posts and the area centres a great deal of extra work and responsibility. It was not a clear-cut question of one air war ending and another beginning – the two now ran simultaneously.

At the time of the flying-bombs, the Allied air offensive had actually been directed very much against Germany itself. The RAF had for some time been carrying out massive raids, mainly at night, against German industrial and other targets, a campaign that, from 1943, had been backed by daylight raids by the United States Army Air Force, flying from Britain. Germany needed a way of striking back at the British Isles without committing her all too few remaining bombers. One result was the invention and development, after many experiments and tests, of the V1. This consisted of a torpedo-shaped fuselage supporting square-cut wings and tailplane, with a pulse-jet engine mounted above and to the rear. These weapons were designed to fly without a pilot, and carried a high-blast-effect warhead in the nose, which also contained a range-setting cutout device and a simple magnetic/gyroscopic guidance system. Huge ramps were erected up which the projectiles were launched, propelled initially by a steam-powered trolley. V1 production became big business for Germany, and by December 1943 the flying-bombs were being churned out at the rate of between 1,200 and 1,400 a month. By June 1944 the

ROC visit to Greenham Common in July 1944. C/Obs S. Jewell (7th from L standing), Obs (W) Y. Copper (4th from R standing), L/Obs J. Wedge (5th from left front row), all others unknown. (ROCM/Stan Jewell)

Group Captain Tom Gleave
CBE FRHistS FCGA RAF (Rtd.)

In February 1923 an air defence plan for
London which encroached on the immediate
surrounding counties was produced. Among its
main features was an Advanced Observer Post
belt running through all the surrounding
counties and sandwiched between an Aircraft
Fighting Zone and a coastwise locator belt.
Further developments resulted in the
elimination of the locators and in the
formation of the Observer Corps (later The
Royal Observer Corps) and the extension of its
area of operations to the coast. When the
coastwise Radar screen came into operation the
Observer Corps filled the gap in enemy
aircraft detection between the coastwise
inward limit of radar detection and the
enemy's chosen targets. This was achieved and
in excellent working order in time for the
Battle of Britain. No more richly deserving
claim can be made on behalf of the Observer
Corps as it was then that it was a vital cog
in the machine that crushed the might of the
Luftwaffe at a most critical moment in our
Island History in which it has rightly earned
itself a place.

Above and **Below:** The Royal Observer Corps contingent at the Battle of Britain Salute 26 September 1943, march through Whitehall (above) and past His Majesty the King in front of Buckingham Palace (below). (ROCM/Mrs S. Fulcher) **Inset**: Group Captain Tom Gleave. (Gp Capt Tom Gleave)

numbers had reached 8,000 a month, while a vast network of railways connected the ever-increasing main and reserve launching-sites.

The German plan was to mount such a heavy bombardment of south-east England that British and American resources would have to be distracted from preparations for the inevitable invasion; large raids by Luftwaffe bombers would be combined with massive V1 attacks. Unfortunately for the Germans, however, the RAF and USAAF bombers were one step ahead, and had little difficulty in destroying the launching-sites which, with their long fixed ramps, stood out like sore thumbs. For this and other reasons the V1 attacks were delayed, and the Allied invasion took place on 6 June 1944, though Germany still went ahead with a disastrous series of air attacks against Britain, which cost the Luftwaffe dearly. During the muddled V1 offensive, which, as has been said, began in June 1944, the majority of the weapons were launched from an area between Dunkirk and Rouen on the French coast, and most Royal Observer Corps identifications were made between Dymchurch and Beachy Head. There was one advantage in the tracking of a flying-bomb, in that they steered a straight course, with just an occasional deviation to left or right just prior to impact. Their air-speed ranged from between 240 and 400 mph, and most flew at heights between 1,000 and 3,000 feet. These pilotless aircraft were given various nick-names in England, notably 'buzz-bombs' and 'doodlebugs'.

From the start of the German offensive, it was painfully clear that London was the main target for Hitler's new 'revenge weapons'. As there was no element of precision involved in this type of bombing, the V1s served very little military purpose. The simple truth was that the Nazis were indiscriminately bombing civilian centres, in a bid to destroy the morale of the people and to tie down a great amount of Allied resources. In the very first raid on 13 June, three V1s reached London. One of them exploded in Bethnal Green and killed six people, though luckily, the other two caused no further casualties. Two days later, on the 15th, the Germans sent wave after wave across the Channel. One hundred and forty-four V1s crossed the English coast, seventy-two of which exploded in London, and the day later became known as 'The Battle of London.'

Ivor Matanle's book *World War II* describes something of the air defence structure at that time:

The Commander of 12 Group RAF, Air Marshal Roderic Hill, now faced a major task, quite unlike any that Fighter Command RAF had faced previously. He put into action Operation Overlord/Diver, an extensively planned defence exercise designed to combat pilotless bombs with RAF fighter aircraft in close co-operation with Anti-Aircraft Command and Balloon Command. Eight day-fighter squadrons - flying Spitfires, Tempests and Typhoons - and four Mosquito night-fighter squadrons were allotted to the task of destroying the flying-bombs. To them, in August 1944, would be added the first of the Gloster Meteor I jet fighters, the Allies' first operational jet aircraft.

Britain's radar defences once again proved inadequate in the face of these new weapons, and the major workload of detecting and monitoring them fell to the Royal Observer Corps. The V1 main flight-path passed through an area which became infamously known as 'Doodlebug Alley', and the three groups primarily involved in plotting the bombs' courses were Horsham, Maidstone and Bromley. Quite a few V1s got as far as Watford and Colchester Groups, while Winchester Group also had its own problem as the German High Command had pin-pointed Southampton as one of its targets.

The Observer Corps' chief advantage over radar was in the certainty with which they could identify the V1s; there were, after all, no other machines in the sky that remotely resembled them either in appearance or sound. Radar, however, had no way of identifying the incoming signal as a V1, an enemy aircraft, or a friendly one. It was impracticable to scramble fighters on the receipt of every radar signal, since to have done so would have been a vast waste of manpower and vital materials. Once again, therefore, as the eyes and ears of Britain, the Royal Observer Corps proved to be an enormous asset. By day an observer could identify a doodlebug by sight, and in bad weather, or at night, there was no mistaking the machine's unique sound. With the RAF controllers posted at Observer Corps operations rooms, enabling them to scramble fighters directly from ROC plotting tables, Horsham and Maidstone Groups were instrumental in the destruction of over 200 flying-bombs.

Although British radar had proved inadequate, the Americans had developed a low-level radar system known as MEW (Microwave Early Warning), which they loaned to the British air defence and which was deployed at Fairlight in Sussex on 29 June 1944. This radar system had direct links with the ops rooms at both Horsham and Maidstone. The MEW only remained in operation for two months, but in that short time it was responsible for 142 V1 kills. MEW was replaced by the British Type 26 radar, which was very similar to the American equipment. But, however good the kill figures may seem, they were still only the tip of the iceberg, though Britain was at least now protected by a radar system which could reliably pick up flying-bombs as they approached from across the sea.

Royal Observer Corps posts along the coastline were issued with Snowflake/Totter rockets, which were fired on making a positive sighting of a flying-bomb within two miles of a post. The benefit of the Snowflake rockets was that they alerted any fighter patrol aircraft in the vicinity to the location of an incoming doodlebug. Other defences against the flying-bomb included a balloon barrage and an anti-aircraft gun belt from Beachy Head to Dover.

The main problem that the RAF had at the start of the attacks was the fact that the V1s were both too fast, and much too small a target, for Spitfires and Typhoons. Even the newly introduced Hawker Tempest V, which had a maximum speed of 436 mph, found the targets difficult to intercept. Ivor Matanle goes on to explain how the disadvantage was overcome:

However, the RAF pilots devised a precision flying technique by which the airflow over the upper surface of a Tempest's wing, positioned only inches below the wing of the flying-bomb, disturbed the aerodynamic performance of the V1's wings sufficiently to tip the bomb over and send it crashing into the sea. In one way or the other, RAF fighters, mainly Tempests, accounted for more than a third of the V1s that were destroyed before they reached London and its suburbs.

Another problem with shooting down the V1s above London was that they still fell, either as debris or as unexploded warheads, into the populous areas. By late June it was decided to move London's anti-aircraft defences 20 miles south of the city to the North Downs, and the job of co-ordinating the defences against the flying-bombs was given to Winston Churchill's son-in-law, Duncan Sandys, who at the time was Parliamentary Secretary to the Ministry of Supply. Again from Ivor Matanle's book we learn:

The Crossbow Committee [the name given to the War Cabinet Committee for defence against the flying-bombs and V2 rockets, of which Sandys was Chairman] recommended the bold step of moving the anti-aircraft defences to the coast, where the newly available American proximity-fused shells could safely be used against flying-bombs approaching from the sea. These shells exploded only if close to their target, so fell back to earth unexploded if badly aimed. As a result, they could not safely be used over land. In only four days, four hundred heavy anti-aircraft guns and six hundred Bofors guns were moved and re-sited. Three thousand miles of telephone cable were laid, and twenty-three thousand personnel were relocated.

Up until September 1944 Germany had launched 9,000 V1s against London and a further fifty-three against Southampton – at a rate of one launch every one and a half hours, though the actual destruction that they caused was greatly reduced by the fact that at least 1,000 of them crashed shortly after take-off. The defences shot down 3,463, 3,262 crashed over Britain, and 2340 reached London.

After Allied invasion troops had captured the V1 launching-sites in France, the offensive continued from Holland. For a time the weapons were air-launched from the wings of Heinkel He111 bombers. This phase lasted until February 1945, when Germany, in desperation, fired new long-range V1s from bases inside Holland. The last flying-bomb

Above left: Obs Jim White, C/Obs Percy Smith, Obs Harry Spratt and Obs (W) Vivien Paris, carry out aircraft plotting on Fordingbridge post in 1953. (ROCM/Henry Wills) **Above right:** Geoff Rice, Dr. Sir Barnes Wallis and Dave Shannon at the ceremony at Middle Wallop in May 1975 when the rebuilt (Dambuster) mine was handed over to 617 Squadron by 14 Group ROC. Mr Rice and Mr Shannon were ex aircrew of 617. (ROCM/Henry Wills)
Below: Stand-down photograph from Longparish post. Rear from left to right: Obs B. Kelly, A. Groves, A. Webb, R. Dobson, A. Turton, R. Mills, W. Sands. Centre: Obs P. Hounsome, W. Walker, F. Stanard, G. Alexander, A. Wedge, W. Lywood, A. Powell, L. Turton, F. Worthington. Front: Obs (W) G. Worthington, C/Obs A. Snow, Obs Lt K. Cable, L/Obs R. Snow, Obs (W) P. Powell. (ROCM/Mrs K. Belton)

to explode on British soil did so on 29 March 1945 at Datchworth, near Hatfield.

Hitler's next revenge weapon was, of course, the V2, a rocket that could lift off vertically and flew faster than the speed of sound; in addition, it did not need the large permanent launching-ramps that the V1 required. Unfortunately, the defences could do little about them. It was impossible for fighter aircraft to chase, catch and destroy them, and equally impossible to track them by any means then available. They were unlike anything that had gone before, but luckily their reign of terror only lasted for the six months between September 1944 and March 1945. Within that short time, however, they were to cause the deaths of nearly 3,000 people in Britain.

Royal Observer Corps HQ at Bentley Priory came through the war with very little damage, which is particularly surprising given the importance of the building in its various guises. Two small bombs destroyed a wooden hut and a flying-bomb smashed a few windows. A V2 also landed in the vicinity, though it caused little more damage than to smash a few window panes in the Ante-Room.

Air Chief Marshal Sir Roderic Hill was to pay the corps a great compliment in his official report on the flying-bomb campaign: 'The part played by the Royal Observer Corps - the silent service of the air defences - was an epic in itself.' And on 11 July 1944, C. S. Petheram, Principal Assistant Secretary, Ministry of Home Security, addressed a letter to the Commandant of the Royal Observer Corps which read:

The recent attacks by flying-bombs over South-East England and the London area have tested to the utmost the new system of national air-raid warnings and the industrial warning system in that area. This experience has shown that both the national and the local warning systems have come through this testing period well. Generally the public and the factories have confidence in the warnings given by Ministry of Home Security officers and this reflects great credit not only on the officers who give the warnings but also on those who have provided the information and the communications on which the system of warnings depends. The detection and plotting of flying-bombs by the Royal Observer Corps have been excellent and the work of the General Post Office on communications has been of the high standard we now expect. I am glad to tell you that, in answering questions in the House of Commons on July 6th, the Minister of Home Security said:- 'But my own personal view is that, taking it by and large, the warning system is working to the general satisfaction. It is a complicated business, highly controversial. The alarm within the alert, for instance has been a most valuable thing; and, if I may take the unusual course of saying so, I would like to pay tribute to the officers of my Department, the Royal Observer Corps and the General Post Office.'

Bratton post manned by Observers Charlie Lawrence and Fred Davis after the Second World War. Note metal tripod and post instrument but no structure. (ROCM/Obs Off B. Davis)

CHAPTER SEVEN
Re-formation of
the Royal Observer Corps

In his message to the Royal Observer Corps in May 1945, not long after Germany had surrendered, Air Chief Marshal Sir Roderic Hill (as he had now become), Air Officer Commanding-in-Chief, Fighter Command, thanked the corps in these terms:

> For nearly six years now the Royal Observer Corps has maintained a continuous lookout on the skies over Britain. This vigil, in magnitude and time, far exceeds any hitherto recorded .... No matter what surprise or what new tactics the enemy has sprung, the Royal Observer Corps has invariably risen to the occasion. Your triumph is the greater because your task has called for the sterner virtues of endurance, self-sacrifice, vigilance and patience of no ordinary kind. Among praiseworthy aspects of your work, I must allude specially to your tracking of friendly aircraft. Outsiders, perhaps, know little of its merits; but the Royal Air Force knows and is grateful. A very large number of aircrews of all Commands owe their lives to your care.

The Second World War finally ended with the Japanese surrender on 14 August 1945. The Royal Observer Corps had the honour of taking part in London's great Victory Parade, but sadly, for them the cheering and applause were quickly to fade away. There no longer seemed any point in maintaining the corps, and it was officially decided that it should be 'stood down'. However, it was not completely disbanded, because the service which the observers provided was now firmly considered to be an essential part of the country's defence system. In January 1947, as the shape of post-war Europe began to emerge, with its threat of nuclear war, the corps was re-formed with Cabinet approval. Air Commodore the Earl of

Above: Kingsworthy post crew in April 1942. Standing left to right: J. Page, B. Banfield, W. Small, T. Cook, E. Dean, L. Hayes, Rev. S. Williams, R. Matcham, A. Lawrence, J. Munns, J. Weeks, C. Hyde, E. Clelford, E. Vokes. Left to right on chairs: R. Snow, C/Obs J. Holdaway, Group Officer unknown, General Sir William Twiss, L/Obs M. Horne. Left to right on ground: M. Simpkins, J. Bulpett. (ROCM/J. Holdaway) **Below:** The same post at Kingsworthy at the time of the stand down in 1945. Rear from left to right: R. Parsons, H. Fowler, T. Cook, C. Hyde, R. Matcham, W. Stacey, A. Stagg, J. Wills, W. Small. Centre: R. Snow, M. Horn, General Sir William Twiss, J. Weeks, E. Vokes, Rev. S. Williams. Front row: A. Eustace, J. Page, J. Bulpett, Mrs Stacey, M. Simpkins, H. Bulpett. These two photographs are a good example of how the general appearance and organisation of the Corps rapidly changed in the 40's. (ROCM/Mrs E. Stagg)

Bandon, who had taken over as Commandant from Air Commodore Finlay Crerar in November 1945, remained in that position to instigate the corps' reformation. Over the next two years the corps was rebuilt, pretty much to the same level and on the same geographical lines as had obtained at the end of the war. Bandon drew upon a considerable number of observers who had served in the war to form the nucleus of the new organization.

In 1948 the very first Royal Observer Corps training camp was held. These camps were designed to give observers, who were now mainly part-timers, a week of intensive training during the summer. The Royal Air Force happily provided the venue at Thorney Island, and summer camps remained with the corps throughout the rest of its history. On 1 February 1949 Bandon relinquished his appointment and it was taken over by Air Commodore R. B. Jordan.

The Royal Observer Corps took yet another step forward when the Air Officer Commanding-in-Chief, Fighter Command, assumed administrative control over it on 1 March 1950. Throughout the Battle of Britain the corps' HQ at Bentley Priory held a position of high importance. As has been said, Fighter Command HQ for the whole of the battle was also at Bentley Priory, under the control of Air Chief Marshal Dowding. A special underground operations block had been built for this purpose, and in 1944 the operations room became the Allied Expeditionary Force War Room, from where General Eisenhower's staff had planned the D-Day landings. Headquarters of the Royal Observer Corps now had a status comparable with that of a Fighter Group HQ.

A new honour was to be bestowed on the Royal Observer Corps on the 11 April 1950. That year was actually the twenty-fifth anniversary of the corps' formation, and to mark the occasion it was announced that His Majesty King George VI would become the first Air Commodore-in-Chief of the corps.

Air Commodore Jordan only stayed as Commandant until 20 March 1951, when he handed over his command to Air Commodore G. H. Vasse.

1953 proved to be an eventful year in the corps' history, as it

Above: Obs J. Gamblin and C/Obs R. Davis leave elevated orlit post at Alderbury in the 1950's with post chart table, log, telephone and fixed-focus binoculars. (ROCM/Henry Wills) **Below:** Plotters around Watford main table pre. 1953. (ROCM/Bedford Group)

Above: Sir Basil Embry the Commander in Chief of Fighter Command reviews the ROC camp at Thorney Island in September 1949. (ROCM/C/Obs S. Jewell)

Below: Bedford Group officers in the early 50's. Rear from left to right: Obs Off S.G. Barnes, Obs Off P. Amos, Obs Lt E.C. Tyrell, unknown. Front from left to right: unknown, Obs Lt H. Crawley, Obs Lt R.A. Grimmer, Obs Cdr H.A.N. Tebbs, Obs Lt Griggs, Obs Lt E.C. Clifton. (ROCM/Bedford Group)

did for the rest of the country. With the death of King George VI in February 1952, his daughter and successor to the throne, Queen Elizabeth II, assumed the appointment of Air Commodore-in-Chief, Royal Observer Corps, the appointment taking effect from the moment of her coronation on 2 June 1953. Her Majesty the Queen may well have had a lot of titles thrust upon her at that time; indeed, to some people, the association between her titles and the organizations to which they belong might appear a trifle impersonal. Where the Royal Observer Corps was concerned, however, this was certainly not the case. During the Second World War, the then Princess Elizabeth had had a number of encounters with the corps. Windsor Castle itself had its own post, situated on the Brunswick Tower, to which both the Princess and her father, the King, made a number of visits. One famous story tells of events at the post on 18 June 1944. On the night in question the post was manned by Observer F. R. Hazell and the Reverend D. Southeard. It was a beautifully clear evening, so much so that both St Paul's Cathedral and Big Ben, 22 miles away, could be clearly seen. Hitler's V1 campaign had started in earnest and the observers' activities centred around the plotting of a dozen flying-bombs, many of which crashed within sight of the post. One of the Royal pages appeared from the castle and informed Hazell and Southeard that King George and Queen Elizabeth would be paying them a visit in exactly one minute's time; the Royal party would also include Princess Elizabeth and the Hon. Andrew Elphinstone, the Queen's nephew. Observer Hazell showed them all his pack of aircraft recognition cards and, to his great surprise, the King and Princess Elizabeth could between them identify nearly every one. During the visit the Princess apparently looked up and said, 'Are you going to plot that Wellington?' Looking through their binoculars, Hazell and Southeard confirmed, with some embarrassment, that there was indeed a Wellington overhead, and hurriedly relayed a message to their centre (probably Watford): 'Wellington over post - north-east - one at nine.' Their embarrassment was short-lived, however, as a couple of flying-bombs crashed in the vicinity, making everyone present don their steel helmets with all due haste.

Also in 1953, it was decided to extend the Royal Observer Corps' field of operations to Northern Ireland, by creating a new group with its headquarters at Belfast.

This period of the corps' history wasn't all plain sailing. The fact that aircraft were continually being designed that could reach ever-increasing operating speeds and heights, put a question mark over the efficiency of the organization. A number of revisions to the corps' operational layout were considered and a series of changes took effect from 1 November 1953. There were two main objectives behind these revisions. First, as the boundaries of the Fighter Command sectors had already undergone substantial revision, it was planned to rearrange the ROC group and area boundaries to coincide with these. Secondly, it was decided to improve the handover tracks from group to group by increasing the size of groups and providing additional facilities. Because of the rearrangement of the area boundaries Midland Area was split into two, now becoming Northern and Eastern Areas. Things became a little confusing when Southern Area was renamed Metropolitan Area, Western Area became Southern Area, and North-Western Area became Western Area. While all this might sound like a huge game of musical chairs, the idea was to give all Royal Observer Corps groups the same boundaries and names as the Fighter Command sectors to which they were affiliated. The only area where this scheme didn't apply was in Scotland. Scottish Area was allowed to keep its original name, but its boundaries were made to conform with the Caledonian Fighter Command sector.

The only way in which the corps could enlarge the areas covered by each group was by making a reduction in the number of groups. When the stand-down had been announced at the end of the war, the Royal Observer Corps boasted a network of forty groups; in 1953, after the creation of the Belfast Group, it once again stood at its wartime strength. It was now decided to slash the number of groups to only thirty-one. Nine operations rooms were phased out, these being Lincoln, Bury St Edmunds, Cambridge, Gloucester, Cardiff, Wrexham,

Dunfermline, York 9 and, most surprisingly of all, Maidstone – Maidstone and Horsham had been the two busiest operations rooms in the country throughout the war years. With the closure of York 9, the two York groups merged and were directed from the operations room belonging to York 10, which also became the area headquarters of the newly formed Northern Area. The posts that had reported to the now redundant operations rooms had their communications links redirected to another group headquarters. Measures to improve track handover were also put into operation. Post clusters were designed to straddle group boundaries, so that reports could be received simultaneously at both operations rooms, while open liaison lines between groups meant that fast-flying aircraft could be 'talked over' group boundaries.

Air Commodore Vasse handed over the Commandant's mantle to Air Commodore J. H. T. Simpson on 29 March 1954.

CHAPTER EIGHT
The Royal Observer Corps in the Nuclear Age

Since the end of the Second World War there had been an uneasy peace between the former allies who together had defeated Nazi Germany. By the late 1940s the Soviet Union had come to be considered as the natural enemy of the western democracies, and measures had to be adopted to protect Britain against the nuclear threat Russia and her satellite nations posed. The nuclear issue did not really raise its head until about 1947. The United States was then quite openly continuing its development of atomic weapons, and all the evidence suggested that the Soviet Union had its own intensive programme of research into similar weapons. Britain began its own research and development programme in October 1947. In 1948 the four main powers that had been allies during the Second World War – Britain, France, Russia and the USA – held a conference to decide the future of Germany. It was then that the Cold War began in earnest. The Soviet Union systematically set about closing all of its road and rail communications with the West.

In 1955 it was decided that the Royal Observer Corps would be the ideal organization to deal with the detecting, measuring and reporting of the radioactive fallout that would inevitably result from the use of nuclear weapons. The ROC network was the obvious choice for taking on the work that the National Warning Organisation (which is described later in this chapter) had in mind, which was to gather the information to provide warnings to both service and civil authorities. The corps had posts situated near to virtually every main settlement in the country. In the eventuality of a nuclear strike on this country it would no longer be a question of warning just the major cities and large factories against air attack, for nuclear fallout would be indiscriminate and could effect every corner of the British Isles, from the centre of London to the most remote Scottish valley. It was hoped that every single citizen of Great Britain could be warned and kept updated on the situation around the country, or just locally, by the information that the Royal Observer Corps would provide to them indirectly. Training for the corps' new role began on 3 October 1955. It is, of course, to be remembered that at this stage the corps was still employed in its original duties of aircraft recognition; the nuclear fallout role would be an additional task, although it became apparent from the very start that it was considered to be the more important of the two.

Because of the nature of the work, over the next few years the corps had to undergo a complete transformation. The most obvious problem with the existing system was the structure of the posts and centres themselves. Observing incoming aircraft from a raised observation post that was very much open to the elements may have served a useful purpose during the war, but faced with a possible nuclear attack such posts would have been totally useless. A massive building plan would therefore

At the Battle of Britain Exhibition in London Airport in 1957, Leading Observer Huntley of Acton is seen handling a model of Fairey Delta 2 WG774. (ROCM/Obs Cdr G.A.D. Bourne)

have to be implemented to construct and equip new posts all round the country. During this building programme, which began in 1957, the opportunity was taken to resite many of the operations rooms and posts. As far as posts were concerned, what was needed was a protected bunker from which a crew of observers could carry out observations for an unspecified period of time. If fallout did occur near a post, the observers on duty could hardly pack up and go home. The crew would have to remain at the post to monitor the fallout around them, reporting their information to their operations room, where other crews would have to stay until such a time as it was deemed safe to leave the building. It was recognised that it could take at least a couple of weeks for the air outside to clear sufficiently for the crew on duty to be relieved. It was essential, therefore, that both post and centre could remain self-sufficient for however long the danger might last. Posts had to be built underground, and needed to be blast-proof and protected against fallout. They needed sleeping accommodation, generators for their own electricity supply, sanitation and ventilation, as well as being stocked with all manner of supplies and equipment. The first protected post was built in June 1956 at Farnham in Surrey, after rigorous tests and experiments. The equipment to be used at posts, and the procedure that observer crews should adopt, all derived to a considerable extent from the tests carried out at Farnham. The experiments proved to be so successful that the subsequent building programme was almost complete by the end of 1963, with an estimated 250 posts a year then being built. Posts were formed into 'clusters' of two or three linked together, and also linked to their group control by land-line communication. Where the possibility of nuclear attack – rather than conventional air attack – was concerned, there was no necessity to straddle posts across group boundaries, and so post crews only needed to report directly to their own group operations room.

Each group headquarters also had to be protected against blast and be self-sufficient for long periods of time. Many wartime sites that could be easily adapted were made available to the Royal Observer Corps. No 12 Group Bristol and No 31

Above: **left:** Post Chief Observer operating the LUWA Ventilator. (ROCM/Metropolitan Area) **Above right:** The Commandant's driver (?) descending the ladder into the prototype post at Farnham in August 1956. (© Crown copyright 1993/MOD reproduced with the permission of the Controller of HMSO) **Below:** Post plotters entering readings on post boards at Horsham control. (© Crown copyright 1993/MOD reproduced with the permission of the Controller of HMSO)

Group Belfast moved into converted and disused anti-aircraft operations rooms. Further conversions were made at No 30 Group Inverness and No 21 Group Preston, where disused RAF sector operations centres were found to be suitable. All other groups were provided with brand-new purpose-built group headquarters buildings. There were two types of design used for these complexes: basically, semi-sunk and surface. The first two were completed in 1960 at Fiskerton for the Lincoln Group and at Wrexham for the North Wales Group; Fiskerton was a semi-sunk complex and Wrexham a surface one.

Air Commodore J. M. Warfield succeeded Air Commodore Simpson as Commandant of the corps on 4 May 1959. Also in 1959, the government of the Isle of Man gave the go-ahead for a cluster of four posts to be built on the island. These posts became part of No 22 Group Carlisle and made their reports directly to the English mainland. In 1960 the Royal Observer Corps was to reach the Scottish islands, when twenty-five posts were built on Orkney, Shetland and in the Hebrides.

Winchester Centre Long Range Board 1958. Left to right: Obs (W) J. Smith, Obs (W) D. Ruffel-Hazel, Obs unknown, Obs (W) D. Hayes, C/Obs P. Mulvey, Obs (W) unknown, C/Obs (W) B. Newman. (ROCM)

For a number of reasons the Royal Observer Corps had always been an evolving organization. Now, with all the changes that were being made to accommodate their new role, it was an ideal time to reorganize the groups even further. As had been the case quite often in the past, it was mainly the boundaries of groups that changed. For instance, in Western Area, the northern part of No 19 Group Manchester was amalgamated with the biggest part of No 21 Group Lancaster. This created a new 21 Group, to be called Preston, for which, as has been said, a new group headquarters had already been designed and converted from a disused sector operations centre. The now redundant HQs at Manchester and Lancaster became secondary operations rooms within Preston Group. In Scotland, No 26 Group Glasgow was disbanded altogether and its posts were divided up between No 25 Group Ayr, No 27 Group Oban and No 28 Group Dundee. In Northern Area, No 18 Group Leeds was reduced in size and No 20 Group York and No 23 Group Durham were enlarged to compensate.

On 29 May 1961, Air Commodore Warfield relinquished his appointment as Commandant of the Royal Observer Corps and was succeeded by Air Commodore C. M. Wight-Boycott.

To understand the direction that the Royal Observer Corps was now taking, it is necessary to know something of the United Kingdom Warning and Monitoring Organization (UKWMO). During the Second World War and at the time of the reorganization just after the war, the information the corps provided was primarily for the benefit of the various Fighter Command groups. However, in its new role of detecting and measuring radioactive fallout, the corps' operational capabilities were designed to facilitate the work of the UKWMO, which had been established with five primary objectives: 1) to originate warnings of the threat of air attack; 2) to provide confirmation of nuclear strike; 3) to originate warnings of the approach of radioactive fallout; 4) to provide regional government headquarters, local authority emergency centres (LAECs), and certain armed service headquarters in the United Kingdom, offshore islands and neighbouring countries, with details of nuclear bursts and with a scientific appreciation of the path and intensity of fallout; 5) to provide an emergency meteorological service post-attack.

The Royal Observer Corps was officially the field force of the UKWMO, responsible for the collection, movement, processing and further movement of data. The UKWMO was split into sectors, the boundaries of which corresponded to those of the ROC areas. Each sector had a sector control, which would be located at the same premises as one of the Observer Corps group headquarters within that particular area.

To enable the corps to provide an effective service, each post had to be equipped with a range of highly specialized equipment, which will be described later (see Chapter Nine), and the massive task of equipping every post reached its climax in 1962. It was now decided to take a critical look at the system of communication between posts and their groups. The existing telephone system was by no means perfect, since if any problems arose on the line, or the line was broken, the posts would be unable to relay their information. It was therefore decided to provide one post in each cluster with a radio, such posts then being termed Radio Posts. Since each cluster already had a Master Post, which was equipped with weather-forecasting equipment that the other posts did not have, the ideal solution was to equip the Master Post with the radio, so making it by far the most important post in the cluster. This meant that if, for any reason such as the blast of a bomb, the telephone communications were to be severed, at least one post in each cluster could still transmit its reports to the respective group headquarters. Trials for this system were held in No 14 Group Winchester in 1962, and proved so successful that a programme was drawn up to equip the other groups.

Air Commodore J. H. Greswell became Commandant of the corps on 3 June 1964, taking over from Air Commodore Wight-Boycott. Also in that year, a working party was established to investigate the feasibility of using teleprinter transmission to replace speech telling of information between groups, between groups and sectors, and so on. No 1 Group's secondary training base at Beckenham was the location for the teleprinter transmission experiments. The results were

Above: Visit to Alderbury post in April 1962 by Councillor H. Kidwell, the Mayor of Salisbury. Looking on are Obs Cdr W. Belton (right) and Obs J. Abbott (left). (ROCM/Henry Wills) **Below left:** Radio Aerial trials at Alderbury post with C/Obs R. Davis (foreground) and Obs Searle. (ROCM/Henry Wills) **Below right:** C/Obs Phil Mulvey manning the Post Controller position at 14 Group Centre in July 1962. (ROCM)

successful, and the go-ahead was given in 1965 to equip all of the groups that covered south-east England – Nos 1, 2, 4 and 5 – with the system, with the rest of the country to follow suit in due course.

In 1965 the corps' air recognition duties were finally wound down. As the nuclear threat to the country grew in size and complexity, so the consideration that the Royal Observer Corps could play any role in a future air war diminished. The speed of modern aeroplanes was such that positive identification by sight was highly questionable. During the war it had been possible to pick up a German aircraft as soon as it crossed the coast, and then plot its course and direct the air defences against it. By 1965, however, this all seemed a little impractical; after all, an attacking enemy aircraft could have entered British airspace, flown to London, dropped its bombs and returned, while observers were still deciding whether it was friend or foe. In a new directive to the Corps Commandant, the Air Officer Commanding-in-Chief, Fighter Command, stated that there was no current operational requirement for aircraft reporting by the Royal Observer Corps. Training in aircraft recognition did continue, however, as there was always a possibility that

Tellers at Winchester Control in 1964. Right to left: Joe Spicer (Chief Warning Officer), Obs Lt Les Tipping, C/Obs (W) E. Jeffery, C/Obs C. Forester, Obs (W) M. Fourt, Obs (W) J. Smith, Obs (W) R. Butler, Obs Matcham. (© Crown copyright 1993/MOD reproduced with the permission of the Controller of HMSO)

Above: The Commander in Chief of Fighter Command, Sir Dermott A. Boyle, inspects ROC camp models at RAF Stradishall in 1955. Also present are Air Commodore J. Simpson and Observer Commander D. Miller. (© Crown copyright 1993/MOD reproduced with the permission of the Controller of HMSO)

Below: Women's flight march off from RAF West Malling parade ground at the start of another busy camp day in July 1958. (ROCM/C/Obs (W) Rita Cullingford)

Above: Air Vice Marshal Robertson reviews the women's flight at RAF
Newton in 1964. (ROCM/C/Obs (W) Rita Cullingford)
Below: Master test in Civil Defence Centre, Parchment Street, Winchester
1960s. Left to right: C/Obs P. Mulvey, C/Obs R. Pitman, L/Obs L.
Cresswell, Obs Off D. Alford, Obs (W) R. Cullingford, Obs J. Pitfield,
unknown, C/Obs A. Dowland, L/Obs N. Cullingford, C/Obs McGeary.
(ROCM)

the corps' skills would be called upon in times of emergency. However, the job was now the domain of the more sophisticated technology-based types of early warning systems becoming available to the defences. To compensate for this loss of one of the corps' original roles, there was no let-up in the training for a possible nuclear strike. Nuclear burst reporting was introduced at the posts, and Nuclear Reporting Cells (NRCs) were established in the Air Defence Operations Centre of Fighter Command and other RAF operations rooms.

More changes to ROC group boundaries also took place in 1965. No 23 Group Durham was transferred to Western Area, and the remaining two groups of Northern Area were combined with the four of Eastern Area to form a new Midland Area, Eastern Area then being disbanded. Nos 3 and 14 Groups were transferred from Southern Area to Metropolitan Area.

The Royal Observer Corps continued to hold its annual series of training camps, as it had every summer since 1948. In each

Inside Elstree post, a typical ROC underground post in 1965. (© Crown copyright 1993/MOD reproduced with the permission of the Controller of HMSO)

case the RAF provided the venue, as follows: 1948 and 1949, Thorney Island; 1950 to 1954, Waterbeach; 1955, Stradishall; 1956, Wattisham; 1957, Tangmere; 1958 and 1959, West Malling; 1960 and 1961, Binbrook; 1962, Horsham St Faith; 1963, West Raynham; 1964, Newton; and 1965, Weeton.

1966 proved to be different, however. This was a special year in the corps' history and no summer camp was held; instead, a Royal Review took place at RAF Bentley Priory, Stanmore. The occasion was to mark the twenty-fifth anniversary of the assumption of the style and title 'Royal'. On 24 June 1966 Her Majesty Queen Elizabeth II, the Air Commodore-in-Chief of the Royal Observer Corps, presented the ROC with its Banner, in recognition of the corps' long service and achievements. The blue banner, square in shape, depicted in the centre the badge of the Royal Observer Corps, a beacon-lighter from the times of the first Queen Elizabeth, over the corps' motto, 'Forewarned is Forearmed'. In the upper corner nearest the banner pole was embroidered the Royal Cypher, a crown surmounting the letters EIIR.

At Bentley Priory that day there was a parade of 103 officers and 653 observers drawn from all groups. The parade was commanded by Observer Captain W. Rusby, the Deputy Commandant of the Royal Observer Corps, and Air Commodore Greswell, the Commandant, handed the Banner to the Queen after it had been dedicated by the Chaplain in Chief, Royal Air Force. Her Majesty then presented the Banner to Observer Officer J. D. Ballington, who acted as the Banner Bearer during the review. The Commandant in turn presented the Queen with a jewelled brooch, also in the form of the corps' badge, on behalf of the entire organization, as a statement of their loyalty and in grateful thanks for the presentation of the Banner. The Banner was marched in slow time to the front of the parade as the Central Band of the RAF played the National Anthem; then, during the Royal Salute and the three cheers that followed, the Banner was unfurled and lowered. Following the formality of the parade, Her Majesty walked freely around Bentley Priory's sports field, where she mingled with and talked to many of the 1,500 officers, observers and guests who

Above: HM The Queen, escorted by Air Commodore Greswell, Obs Capt Rusby, and Captain Charles Howard inspecting Watford contingent of the Guard of Honour at RAF Bentley Priory 26 June 1966. (ROCM/Obs Cdr Peter Reeve)

Below: Members of the ROC pose at Bentley Priory during the 1966 Royal Review. Left to right: Obs Henry Wills, C/Obs Bob Symons, Obs (W) May Kiddle, Obs Bob Shergold, Obs D.C. Simmonds, Obs Roy Coulson. (ROCM)

had been invited to celebrate the occasion.

The Banner was thereafter kept at Bentley Priory but was released on very special occasions, such as the last day of summer camps, which were traditionally reviewed by a guest VIP. This VIP may have been a politician, such as the Home Secretary, a senior ranking member of the RAF, or the Commandant of the corps itself. Whenever the Banner was paraded it was accompanied by a guard of honour. The author once himself had the honour of participating in these guard of honour duties. This

Obs Henry Buckton (the author) takes part in the 1986 Guard of Honour at Newcastle-upon-Tyne and is seen here talking with the Commandant, Air Commodore Broughton. (HQ ROC)

particular occasion was the last day of the 1986 summer camp at the University of Newcastle-upon-Tyne, and the reviewing officer was the then Commandant, Air Commodore J. Broughton.

During the 1966 review at Bentley Priory, the Queen made mention of the corps' Royal title, which the Review itself celebrated:

During the Second World War thousands of volunteer members of the Corps maintained continuous watch over the sky of Great Britain, by day and night, in all weathers, from its call-out day on 24 August 1939 until stand-down with victory on 12 May 1945. This was a vital service and it was

107

Above: Banner bearer and escort at RAF Honington 1968. Left to right: Obs J. Barnes, Obs Off G. P. Hounsome, C/Obs K. Reeves, Obs T. Smith. (ROCM)
Below: Inspection of Womens Flight at Middle Wallop May 1975. Right to left: Obs (W) E. Mulvey, unknown, Obs (W) M. Keeping, Obs (W) B. Muchart, C/Obs (W) E. Jeffery, Obs (W) W. Brown, Obs (W) J. Jackson, Obs (W) M. Tormey, unknown, Obs (W) P. Payne, L/Obs C. Forester. Standard Bearer Obs Off M. Walker. VIP's escort Obs Lt L. Tipping, Obs Off (W) B. Newman, Obs Cdr S. Deedman. (ROCM/Henry Wills)

recognised by my father when, after the Battle of Britain, he bestowed on you the title Royal Observer Corps. This well-merited honour was endorsed by the subsequent service of the Corps, both in aiding the offensive operations of the Royal Air Force and in the assistance which it gave in guiding to safety many of our own airmen whose aircraft were in distress.

The Royal Observer Corps was affiliated to the Territorial Army and Volunteer Reserve (TAVR) from 1 April 1968. The date seems a curious one (though it was also the fiftieth anniversary of the formation of the RAF), since in January there had been a major shake-up within the TAVR, one of the measures decided upon by the government to enable major cuts in expenditure within home defence. One is left wondering why the reforms did not lead to disbandment of the corps, instead of affiliation, since under the government cuts the Auxiliary Fire Service, the Civil Defence Corps, and some units of the Territorial Army and Volunteer Reserve were disbanded. It would seem that the Royal Observer Corps' position was secure because of its crucial role within the UKWMO, although the Corps did not altogether escape the knife. Six hundred and eighty-six posts were closed, as were two group headquarters at Watford and Leeds. The Truro and Oban group headquarters, though not actually closed down, became communications centres within other groups, Truro for Exeter, and Oban for Inverness. The manpower of the corps, which had stood at 25,000, was slashed by half, to just 12,500.

RAF Fighter Command, which had stayed in residence at Bentley Priory since the end of the war, amalgamated with Bomber Command on 30 April 1968, to become Strike Command, which had its headquarters at High Wycombe. The Priory became the headquarters of No 11 Group, the operational Air Defence Group of RAF Strike Command, with primary responsibility for the defence of the United Kingdom in wartime and for the integrity of British airspace in peacetime. This amalgamation had no effect on the Royal Observer Corps' status at Bentley Priory, which remained ROC Headquarters.

Air Commodore Greswell was succeeded as Commandant

on 28 June 1968 by Air Commodore D. F. Rixson. Air Commodore Rixson was replaced in turn in January 1971 by Air Commodore E. B. Sismore.

As has been said, one of the functions of the UKWMO was to provide neighbouring countries with details of nuclear bursts and with a scientific appreciation of the path and intensity of fallout. While Air Commodore Sismore was Commandant, he showed a keen interest in visiting some of these countries, and he was able to observe a number of similar organizations on the Continent. One of these organizations was the Ground Observer Corps of the Royal Danish Air Force Home Guard, with which very strong ties were to be made that continued right up until the moment the ROC was stood down.

On 21 March 1945, Squadron Leader Sismore, as he then was, took part in the RAF attack on the Shell Building in Copenhagen, which was being used by the Gestapo as their headquarters in the city. The raid, undertaken at the request of the Danish resistance movement, was a complete success, the eighteen Mosquitoes and their escort of Mustangs demolishing the target. Twenty-six Gestapo agents were killed and all of their files and records destroyed. There were a number of Danish prisoners being held within the building, all of whom escaped during the attack without the loss of a single life, though three Mosquitoes and one Mustang were lost. Sadly, as is the case with many war missions, a tragic accident led to a number of civilian fatalities. One of the Mosquitoes, piloted by Wing Commander P. A. Kleboe, struck one of the uprights of a bridge and crashed into a nearby convent school. When the second wave of bombers arrived on the scene, they mistook the burning convent for the Shell Building and, assuming that the first wave had successfully attacked it, dropped their bombs on the convent, killing 124 children. The pilots who took part in the raid suffered great distress and sorrow as a result of the incident. The Danes, however, hardened by the atrocities committed by the Germans, accepted the accident bravely and acclaimed the attack as a great success and a blow for freedom.

During the commandantship of both Greswell and Sismore, efforts were made to renew links with the RAF, which, inevitably, were becoming ever more distant. The success of these efforts may be measured by people like the author, who served with the corps in the 1980s and who enjoyed a very strong association with the Royal Air Force. During the author's service with the corps a new identity card was designed, the most prominent lettering on which stated that the bearer was a 'Royal Air Force Civilian', and the card was issued under the authority of the Provost-Marshal, RAF.

In May 1973 Air Commodore Sismore handed over as Commandant to Air Commodore R. K. Orrock, DFC. That year was also to witness yet more changes to the group boundaries. Two groups were disbanded altogether, these being No 11 Group Truro and No 27 Group Oban. The future of the these groups had been uncertain ever since 1968, when their group headquarters had been reduced in status. It is necessary to understand, however, that the disbandment of a group was not as serious as it may sound. It was a way of streamlining operations, and although the group headquarters became redundant, the majority of posts would remain operative, reporting to a new group headquarters. The posts that had belonged to Truro were now designated to No 10 Group Exeter, and the Oban posts to No 30 Group Inverness.

1975 was another special year for the Royal Observer Corps, for it marked the Golden Anniversary, celebrating fifty years of service. The main event of the year was a commemorative dinner on 31 October, held in the Officers' Mess at RAF High Wycombe in Buckinghamshire. The guest of honour was again Her Majesty the Queen, the Air Commodore-in-Chief of the Royal Observer Corps, and she was accompanied by His Royal Highness the Duke of Edinburgh. Then, in July of the following year, Queen Elizabeth the Queen Mother attended the Royal Air Force Association Ball, which was held at Bentley Priory. Among the other guests were Group Captain Sir Douglas Bader and Dame Vera Lynn.

1976 saw further success in the attempt to rebuild links between the corps and the RAF. Even though the Air Officer Commanding-in-Chief of Fighter Command had informed the corps as long ago as 1965 that there was no longer an operational requirement for aircraft reporting, it seems that the defence systems were still inadequate in the monitoring of the approach and progress of low-flying aircraft. It was decided to hold tests in October to find out whether or not the Royal Observer Corps would be capable of supplying the RAF defence systems with reliable information about low-flying aircraft. Trials were held at No 15 Group Lincoln and No 6 Group Norwich, and their success was such that the corps was given the opportunity to participate in further tests in 1977, much to the delight of the observers and officers concerned.

In November 1976 Air Commodore M. H. Miller became Commandant of the Royal Observer Corps, taking over from Air Commodore Orrock.

On 4 February 1977 a dinner was held at ROC Headquarters, Bentley Priory, to celebrate the Silver Jubilee of the accession of Her Majesty the Queen – in other words, twenty-five years from her accession and appointment as Air Commodore-in-Chief. The corps presented Her Majesty with a silver model of an Elizabethan beacon lighter, sculpted by Scott Sutherland, bearing a metal plaque inscribed with a message to the Queen from all members of the Royal Observer Corps on the occasion of her Silver Jubilee. Another celebration that took place during 1977 was a Royal Review of Reserve and Cadet Forces at Wembley Stadium on 30 June, which included a contingent from the Royal Observer Corps, and at another Royal Review at RAF Finningley on 29 July, the corps was once again represented.

Also in February 1977, Air Commodore Miller suggested to the Air Officer Commanding No 11 Group, Fighter Command, that the Royal Observer Corps should undertake the task of producing a comprehensive and homogeneous model collection representing all the aircraft types used by the home defence squadrons of the Royal Air Force since its inception in 1918. The collection would be housed at Bentley Priory, where there was already a small model collection. The offer was greatly welcomed, and Flight Lieutenant F. W. T. Davis from Group Operations Staff was nominated as the RAF Project Officer, with the daunting task of compiling a thorough list, in chronological order, of all the aircraft types employed. Observer Lieutenant W. J. E. Manners was appointed Project Officer for the Royal Observer Corps, and decided to establish a common scale of 1:48, and to include major type variations as well as basic types. All in all it was an enormous project. The modellers themselves were volunteers drawn from the ranks of the corps. The first phase of the plan was to construct models from available kits, and the first exhibition was at the corps' 1977 summer camp, held at RAF Cosford. The second phase was the building of models of all the aircraft for which no kits were available. The Bentley Priory model collection is very much a continuing project, and many observers have added their models to it down the years.

Air Commodore Miller was replaced as Commandant in April 1977 by Air Commodore J. F. G. Howe.

In 1979 the United Kingdom Warning and Monitoring Organisation purchased its first microcomputer. This equipment was installed at Oxford, and programmes were designed to help the work of the UKWMO warning teams. Because the Royal Observer Corps acted as the field force of the UKWMO, the computer was also used to help the smooth running of their operations. The purchase of the micro-computer was just one of the measures that were aimed at improving the communications of both the UKWMO and the Emergency Control Network (ECN). It was decided to link sector controls to one another with emergency circuits. In 1980 a system of joining each sector with private wires enabled the installation of telegraph equipment. A Home Defence Review of 1981 looked into ways of improving the communications amongst all the warning organizations, including the corps. The top priority of the review was the improvement of the existing warning system, and by November 1981 all attack warning circuits had been converted to private wires. Every Royal Observer Corps monitoring post was equipped with a carrier receiver, a loudspeaker that could receive attack warning messages. The messages were sent from carrier control points, of which there were 250 throughout the country, situated at major police stations, and these carrier control points were also converted from emergency circuits to private wires. All monitoring posts were issued with loudspeaker telephones, again operating from a private wire instead of emergency circuits, which were used to make contact with the group control on manning up, and to provide information to the group such as the arrival of first fallout, as well as subsequent fallout readings made at five minute intervals. At the same time, much work was also done on creating better radio links between each group control. The posts in Maidstone Group were equipped with new radios, and a programme was drawn up to equip the whole country in due course. 1981 also saw the setting up of a working party with the task of looking into improving the environment within posts; among its targeted areas were ventilation, feeding, lighting and heating. Then, in October, the last secondary training base was closed. Secondary training bases were usually at the site of group headquarters that had been made redundant. The base in question was at Derby, which had been used as a secondary training base since 1953, the year in which Derby Group had become redundant and its posts reallocated.

Air Commodore Howe had relinquished his appointment as Commandant of the Corps in April 1980, and the position was taken over by Air Commodore R. J. Offord.

The working party that had been set up to look at monitoring posts produced its conclusions in 1982. One of its recommendations was that every post should be provided with flooring material; specifically, rolls of strong rubber, which the author can quite clearly remember laying at his own post. For readers who have never seen the inside of a monitoring post, it is quite confined for space – such room as there is is taken up by bunk beds, generators, the operations desk and various other pieces of equipment. As can be imagined, laying the flooring material was therefore no easy task. Each post was issued with five rolls of the new rubber matting for insulating the cold concrete floor, each of which weighed around 30 pounds – collectively, 150 pounds. When it is remembered that many posts were extremely remote, just getting the matting delivered was an epic task. This problem was best demonstrated at Middlesmoor

Post, high in the Yorkshire Dales. The closest road to the post was two miles away in Middlesmoor village, and the observers had to walk the two miles along a dirt track which quite often turned into a river, then across the moors and up to the summit of the hill. Getting the matting to the most accessible of posts was a problem, but to these more remote positions it was a real headache, requiring typical ROC commitment and dedication. The answer was to airlift the matting, and No 3 Flight of the Army Air Corps kindly provided a Gazelle helicopter and crew to lift the five rolls up to Middlesmoor.

In Horsham Group, one of the posts was used to try out a new ventilation fan, and seven-day ration packs were made available to all.

The aircraft recognition question was to surface yet again in 1982. The reader may remember that in 1965 Fighter Command had decided that there was then no necessity for the corps to train in aircraft recognition. Then in 1976 it was decided that there was a need for the corps to report the activities of low-flying aircraft. But in 1982 it was announced that the plotting trials which had begun in 1976 would no longer be continued; the Ministry of Defence could see no further point in the scheme.

In April 1982, however, when Britain assembled its Task Force in response to the invasion of the Falkland Islands by Argentine forces, the Royal Observer Corps made its own contribution. The Argentine Air Force and Naval Air Arm were known to operate both the IA 58 Pucara and the Dassault Super Etendard, two types of aircraft that would undoubtedly be targets for the RAF Regiment's Rapier Squadron, armed with its famous ground-to-air missile. Unfortunately, the problem facing the squadron was that there were no official aircraft recognition filmstrips or slides of either of these aircraft. Because the Task Force had to be assembled and under way with all due haste, solving the problem was a matter of the utmost urgency. Many of the commercial model-making companies were approached to see if they could supply suitable models, but the time needed to complete these models, as well as their cost, were quite unsatisfactory. Someone then had the brainwave of contacting the Bentley Priory model collection, to see if they could supply 1:48 scale models of the Pucara and Super Etendard. The corps rose to the challenge, offering to supply the models in a matter of days, and Bentley Priory immediately set about collecting as much information about their subjects as was available. The research work was done by Observer Lieutenant-Commander Mike Rose and Observer Lieutenant Roy Garwood, who gathered every piece of information they could find into comprehensive data files, which were then sent to the two men who had been asked to make the scale models. This difficult job fell on the shoulders of Observer Byron Scott from No 6 Group and ex-Observer Eric Vine, both of whom had already made contributions to the Bentley Priory model collection. Everybody concerned with the project worked tirelessly around the clock. Two days after ROC Headquarters had first received the request, the models were ready and had been delivered to Bentley Priory. They were next hurried to the Ministry of Defence studios, where they were photographed in various positions and against every conceivable background. After the transparencies had been made, a helicopter flew them aboard the *QEII*, which was just about to set sail for the South Atlantic. During the long voyage to the Falkland Islands the film was used to train members of No 63 Rapier Squadron, RAF Regiment. Further film was made for use by all of the air defence units in the Falklands, and was flown directly to the South Atlantic aboard a Hercules.

In June 1982 Queen Elizabeth the Queen Mother made a return visit to Bentley Priory for a reopening ceremony. Work had begun on renovations to the Priory in the spring of 1979, but on 21 June of that year, while woodwork was being treated with a highly volatile preservative, a fire broke out. The building was very severely damaged. Restoration was a long and difficult undertaking and specialist craftsmen were brought in to restore the Queen Adelaide Room and to replace the ornately carved balustrade of the main staircase.

In February 1983 Air Commodore G. P. Black succeeded Air Commodore Offord as Commandant. On 27 October 1983 His Royal Highness Prince Charles attended a dinner at Bentley

Priory, in celebration of the fortieth anniversary of the first flight of the Gloster Meteor.

In 1981 a microprocessor, which routed messages automatically in conjunction with the existing teleprinter equipment at group controls, was installed at Dundee. This equipment was authorized by the Scottish Home and Health Department after a request from the Director of the United Kingdom Warning and Monitoring Organisation. The existing teleprinter equipment had been designed in the 1960s and, as the Home Office was to agree, the system needed updating. A message switch that could work in conjunction with visual display units and more modern teleprinters was therefore introduced, the first being installed at Maidstone in 1984; when Belfast received the equipment in June the following year, the whole UKWMO network had been standardized. By September 1984, when Air Commodore J. Broughton took over as Commandant from Air Commodore Black, the Royal Observer Corps had reached its peak of operational efficiency.

Air Commodore Broughton was no newcomer to early warning systems. He had been conscripted into the RAF in 1952 as an airman, and in 1953 was granted a National Service

Greenham Common Air Tattoo in 1983. From left to right Observer Lieutenant Commander B.T. Parkes, Air Commodore Black, Observer Officer A. Peach, Woman Observer Officer M. Davidge, Observer Officer C.E.T. Beer and Observer Lieutenant G.P. Hounsome. (ROCM/D. Sharpe)

commission on completion of aircrew training as a navigator and of flying training. He was given a full commission in 1954, and qualified as a Night All-Weather Navigator Radar, seeing service with 125, 89 and 85 Squadrons, RAF. He went on to become an A2 category Fighter Combat Leader on successful completion of graduate training at the Central Fighter Establishment's Fighter Combat School, and joined No 11 Squadron in Germany as Deputy Nav/Rad leader. In 1965 promotion to Squadron Leader gave him a new job as General Duties Training Officer at No 2 Flying Training School, Syerston. In 1969 he was seconded to the Royal Navy to learn about airborne early warning, flying from HMS *Ark Royal*, and in 1972 he helped to introduce the Shackleton AEW aircraft into No 8 Squadron, RAF.

Broughton went on to command No 25 Squadron at Bruggen in Germany, which was equipped with the Bloodhound surface-to-air missile (SAM). On his return to England he became OR 60 (RAF) in the Ministry of Defence responsible for a new airborne early warning project. Promoted Group Captain in 1978, he was appointed OC RAF West Drayton, where the RAF Air Defence Data and London Air Traffic Control Centres are located. His next assignment was at Supreme Headquarters, Allied Powers Europe (SHAPE) in Belgium, as a United Kingdom National Military Representative. In 1983 he returned to the Ministry of Defence as Deputy Director for NATO and Command and Control Policy (RAF). So, when he took over as Corps Commandant in 1984, Air Commodore Broughton had a wealth of experience and knowledge in the field of early warning systems. He was the ideal person to head the corps as it approached its Diamond Jubilee year of 1985 – a year full of change and controversy, and unquestionably one of the most memorable years in the history of the Royal Observer Corps.

CHAPTER NINE
The Warning System

The warning system described in this chapter was operative during the period in which the author served with the Royal Observer Corps, and remained in service until the day the corps was stood down. It is hoped that the reader will by now have concluded from this narrative that the corps was at all times subjected to experimentation and improvement. Even during the author's service in the 1980s, a massive programme was implemented to update all of the equipment used both at the posts and the centres. Group headquarters were brought very much into the computer age, while the equipment used at the posts was updated and made more reliable. The corps manual was rewritten in 1985, and all observers had to hand back their original books in order to be issued with a new A4 ring binder, so designed in order to accommodate any further changes or additions. The warning system that existed in 1985 was therefore a direct result of the years of testing, experiments and building that had gone before.

The Royal Observer Corps was authorized to give a series of three warnings, as well as carrying out its operational duties. These warnings were: air-attack warning RED, meaning imminent danger of attack from the air; fallout warning BLACK, imminent danger of radioactive fallout; and the WHITE warning, the all-clear, signifying safety from the danger of air attack or fallout.

The air-attack warning would originate from United Kingdom Regional Air Operations Centre (UKRAOC), and would be based on information received from all of the allied detection systems, such as the Ballistic Missile Early Warning System (BMEWS). The principal warning officer at UKRAOC would pass the warning to the BBC Central Control to enable an immediate radio message to be broadcast to the nation. It would also relay the warning via a land-line broadcast to the

250 carrier control points installed in major police stations around the country. Obviously, the success of the system relied on the capability of UKRAOC to remain operational during an air attack, although contingency plans did exist to enable certain UKWMO sector controls to receive early warning information and thereafter relay the attack warning themselves.

On receipt of the air-attack warning, the carrier control points would immediately pass a verbal warning along the land-line communications network to the warning points within their area. A warning point was a place where warnings to the public were sounded, and so had to be equipped with a carrier receiver which, as its name suggests, could not relay a message, only receive one. The air-attack warning would be proceeded by a series of high-pitched beeps. There were an estimated 19,000 warning points around the country, situated at police stations, fire stations, coastguard stations, the 870 Royal Observer Corps posts, group headquarters, regional government headquarters, local authority emergency centres, armed service establishments, hospitals, and some industrial and private premises.

When the air-attack warning RED was received at a Royal Observer Corps post, the Number 3 observer would climb through the hatch, taking with him the handle for the siren, which would already have been erected above ground. He would attach the handle and sound the warning, by making a rising and falling note for one minute. There were two types of siren in operation with the corps, the 'Secomak' and the 'Carter', both of which were operated in the same way, though slightly differing in construction.

The siren was kept in the post in a wooden crate and brought to the surface during manning up, assembled (without the handle), and laid on its side close to the post hatch. On top of the siren's sound box was a steadying handle incorporating a twistgrip which opened and closed the damping shutter; to use the siren the shutter would have to be open. To sound attack warning RED, Number 3 observer would have to give five fast rotations of the handle, followed by five slow ones, then five fast, then five slow, and so on for the required minute. This sequence created the warbling, rising-and-falling sound effect that the RED warning needed.

The system was tried and tested, and worked. In fact, during the author's service with the corps, exercises to test the warning system were made at intervals of about two months. During exercises, which were often held during weekends in which a large proportion of NATO's forces would be exercising in the field, the siren procedure was followed exactly. The only difference between practice and the real warning was that observers did not open the damping shutter on the siren during practices, which was quite understandable given that the thing could be heard for many miles.

The fallout warning BLACK was a much more local warning and would be originated at group headquarters. Above ground at every monitoring post there was a piece of equipment called the Ground Zero Indicator (GZI). This was a round box inside of which were four sections. In each of the sections was a cassette containing a piece of printing-out film. The cassettes were positioned within the drum so that one pointed toward the north, one south, one east and one west. If a nuclear bomb exploded, by means of four pin-holes on the drum of the GZI the sensitized paper inside would photograph the image of the fireball and give its elevation on a grid. A second piece of equipment called the Bomb Power Indicator (BPI) would record the peak over-pressure produced by the blast-wave. The BPI measured the blast by means of a metal bellows, one side of which was exposed to normal atmospheric pressure. The blast would cause the bellows to expand and make a reading on the BPI dial, which was situated inside the post itself and showed the pressure on a scale between nought and fifty kilopascals. The post would send its readings from both of these pieces of equipment to group control, where they could be used, in conjunction with reports coming in from other posts in the cluster, to estimate the time of the arrival and the location of radioactive fallout. These predictions had also to rely on meteorological information, since the wind would affect the direction the fallout would take.

The weather information would come from all posts. One

post in each cluster would be equipped with an aneroid barometer, to measure atmospheric pressure in millibars, a hand-held anemometer, which measures wind-speed in knots, and a whirling-frame psychrometer to measure air temperature in degrees fahrenheit. The other posts in the cluster would also make weather reports, though they had no special equipment. These reports had to give wind direction and speed, general weather conditions, and visibility.

When the warning officer at group headquarters decided to send the BLACK warning, he would do so by passing it to the local carrier control points, which in turn forwarded the message to the warning points, from where the warning would be sounded.

The manual states that the BLACK warning should be given by maroon, gong or whistle sounding three bangs or blasts in quick succession. By 1985 the majority of monitoring posts had been issued with maroons, which resembled three small rockets and were launched from a firing-box.

The third warning that a post could make was the WHITE which, as has been said, was basically an all-clear. If the air-attack warning had been sounded but no strike had followed, the UKRAOC would in due course issue the WHITE warning to the carrier control points, which would in turn broadcast it to the warning points. The WHITE warning would also be used in areas that had been affected by radioactive fallout. If the UKWMO and group headquarters agreed with the regional government headquarters and local authority emergency centres that there was no longer any danger from fallout, they would jointly authorize the all-clear on a local basis. At an ROC post the all-clear would be sounded on the siren – this time a steady note of one minute's duration.

The main job of the Royal Observer Corps, other than to sound the three warnings, was to measure gamma radiation dose rate. Following a nuclear strike and the sounding of the RED and BLACK warnings, all corps establishments were designed to close hatches to the outside world and remain self-sufficient until the danger of fallout had passed. In the meantime, the observers within would carry out a scientific study of the intensity of the fallout. The equipment used at posts to measure gamma radiation dose rate was called the Fixed Survey Meter (FSM). A dome above ground would transmit the dose rate down a probe to the liquid crystal display on top of the FSM inside the post, and the reading would also have to be sent to group headquarters, in order to maintain their appreciation of the situation.

At group control rooms, some observers would be engaged in an activity known as triangulation. By using the information supplied by the monitoring posts from their BPIs and GZIs, the group control room observers could determine the position, height and power of a nuclear blast. This information could be checked against the information supplied by AWDREY, Atomic Weapons Detection Recognition and Estimation of Yield, which were nuclear-burst indicators installed at thirteen group controls, each with a minimum range of 75 miles. Between them, these thirteen sites could cover the entire United Kingdom.

At the control room there were basically four display boards or plotting screens, coded A, B, T and E. On Display A was marked the location of all monitoring posts and controls together with group and sector boundaries, the warning districts and the coastline (where appropriate). During an air strike, if contact was lost with a post, a mark was put against it, which would be removed when communications were re-established. Display A was a vertical transparent plotting screen, and three types of information were marked and plotted on the back of it: nuclear burst information, the arrival of first fallout, and the subsequent arrivals of fallout. Display B was another vertical plotting screen, on which nuclear burst information was recorded along with a two-hourly summary of the radiological situation within the group. Every hour, the latest position reached by the fallout from each burst in the area was also indicated on the display. Display T was an opaque plotting screen that provided a nationwide picture of the attack and the resultant fallout threat, while Display E gave an indication of the situation on the continent of Europe.

From 1985 until 1991, when the corps was stood down, the

organization consisted of five areas and a total of twenty-five groups. The five areas were Metropolitan, Midland, Southern, Western and Scottish, each again divided into five groups. The groups in Metropolitan Area were Maidstone No 1, Horsham No 2, Oxford No 3, Colchester No 4, and Winchester No 14. Midland Area consisted of Norwich No 6, Bedford No 7, Coventry No 8, Lincoln No 15 and York No 20. Southern Area consisted of Yeovil No 9, Exeter No 10, Bristol No 12, South Wales No 13, and Shrewsbury No 16. The groups in Western Area were North Wales No 17, Preston No 21, Carlisle No 22, Durham No 23 and Belfast No 31. Scottish Area consisted of Edinburgh No 24, Ayr No 25, Dundee No 28, Aberdeen No 29 and Inverness No 30. Corps Headquarters remained at RAF Bentley Priory, while Metropolitan Area HQ was situated at Horsham, West Sussex; Midland Area at Fiskerton, Lincoln; Southern Area at RAF Rudloe Manor, Hawthorn, Wiltshire; Western Area at Goosnargh, Preston, Lancashire; and Scottish Area at Craigiebarns, Dundee, Angus.

The Royal Observer Corps stood ever ready to spring into action should the situation between the West and the Soviet Union worsen, resulting in a nuclear missile attack on the United Kingdom. In 1985 western Russia was the home of numerous SS-20 missiles. These missiles contained three warheads apiece, and it was not unrealistic to assume that many of them were targeted against the United Kingdom. Britain had little defence against a missile attack, except its Polaris Force, which acted more as a deterrent. Royal Observer Corps journals of the time were still packed with aircraft recognition themes and other airborne headaches, and contained, in particular, all the latest and most up-to-date information about the Soviet air threat (which the author can confirm was pretty fuzzy). The fact remained that a nuclear attack on Britain was more likely to come from air-launched weapons, rather than from ground-launched missiles. The Soviet Long-Range Air Force was equipped with bombers capable of delivering nuclear weapons to Great Britain, and aircraft such as Fencer and Backfire (to give them their NATO code-names) could easily reach the United Kingdom from their bases in western Russia and Poland. One of these aircraft alone could carry twice the bomb-load of a Second World War Lancaster, and they would fly in formations of up to fifty. Whether a nuclear or conventional bombing strike against Britain was contemplated, the initial targets would still be pretty much the same as they were during the Second World War: airfields, radar, and other targets connected with the air defence of the United Kingdom. Group Captain R. A. Masson, Director of Defence Studies, RAF, suggested in an article in the *ROC Journal* that the use of the Soviet Long-Range Air Force with conventional weapons could be attractive to the Soviet Union for three reasons:

First, their new aircraft and stand-off weapons give them such a capability for the first time. Second, the weapons themselves are capable of ever-increasing target accuracy and, third, there may well be less risk of escalation to nuclear warfare from a conventional air attack because of the Soviet's own theatre nuclear superiority and perceived strategic nuclear parity with the United States .... The future [he continued] does not look very encouraging. In 1984 the Soviet Union spent 40% of all its defence expenditure on its air forces. Despite its own economic difficulties, it is continuing to expand its military expenditure each year, now running at some 12% of gross national product per annum of which one fifth is allocated to research and development.

In reassurance, Masson confessed that the United Kingdom was in no imminent danger from Soviet air attack. As far as the Royal Observer Corps was concerned, however, the fact remained that, in 1985, the Soviet Union was capable of the bombing of Britain as well as a nuclear attack, making the operational performance of the corps as critical as it had ever been.

CHAPTER TEN
The Diamond Jubilee

1985 was the Diamond Jubilee of the Royal Observer Corps, marking sixty years of loyal service to Crown and country. It proved to be a very special year in many ways. As has been said, there had already been a number of years that warranted special celebrations during the corps' long history, such as the twenty-fifth anniversary in 1966, when a Royal Review was held at Bentley Priory, and the Golden Jubilee in 1975, when a commemorative dinner was held at RAF High Wycombe in the presence of Her Majesty the Queen. However, the Diamond Jubilee seemed to be the most special of all these occasions. The corps, albeit unknowingly, had very few years to remain operational, and the Diamond Jubilee proved to be a suitable way of saying 'thank you' to all the observers who had come and gone since those long-ago days of 1925. The crowning ceremony of the year was the Royal Garden Party at Bentley Priory, on Thursday 27 June, to which an estimated 2,000 guests were invited. These observers were of every rank, and were chosen from every area and group. Each of the twenty-five groups was represented by a total of forty personnel, made up of the group commandant, deputy group commandant, clerical officer, and thirty-seven officers and observers selected by the group commandant.

An invitation to a Royal Garden Party is an honour cherished by the recipient. Whether one is a royalist or not, the occasion remains one of the most notable experiences in anyone's life, an evergreen anecdote to be retold time and time again with pride (and perhaps an element of smugness). All of which is true of the author who, on this great occasion, had the honour of being the sole representative of his own post. The observers who had been selected to attend the garden party knew nothing about it until an official notification was delivered, by post, from their respective group headquarters, which read: 'I am sure you will be delighted to know that after due consideration, the group commandant has selected you to represent your post at the forthcoming Royal Garden Party in celebration of the Diamond Jubilee.' Next to be issued were the official invitations from RAF Bentley Priory, and a fifteen-page dossier giving details of times, catering, lists of senior personnel, and so on, for the recipient to familiarize himself with. It also included the intended plans of the Queen's movements during the day, both written and illustrated, as well as pointers on dress, saluting and general etiquette. All of this had to be learnt. For instance, when addressing Royalty, if one was lucky enough to get the chance, the conversation should always be opened using 'Your Majesty' or, as appropriate, 'Your Royal Highness'. Thereafter, 'Sir' or 'Ma'am' (with the short 'a', as in 'ham') were to be used. When presented to a Royal visitor, gentlemen were to bow from the neck and ladies curtsy. If wearing uniform headgear one was first to salute. Most important of all, as was explained

Her Majesty the Queen talks with observers from No 9 Group Yeovil during the Royal Garden Party at Bentley Priory 27 June 1985, to mark the Diamond Jubilee. On Her left is Air Commodore Broughton the Commandant, and on Her right, 9 Group Commandant, Obs Cdr H.M. Daniel. (HQ ROC)

to the author by his own group commandant, Observer Commander H. M. Daniel of No 9 Group, 'If you are introduced to Her Majesty as the Archbishop of Canterbury, then for the rest of the visit, that's precisely who you are – you deny nothing.'

All of the representatives were ferried to Stanmore by a fleet of coaches, the Irish and Scottish contingents having been specially flown down for the occasion, though the Yorkshire contingent nearly failed to make it at all, as their coach broke down. The main gates of the RAF station buzzed with both RAF police and civilian police, and there were also a bomb-disposal team and numerous dogs. At the guardroom the coaches were boarded and invitations and identity cards inspected.

Behind the Priory there are two lawns. The higher, nearest to the building, was where Her Majesty the Queen was to meet the selected personnel during a Royal walkabout. Those

On 30 October 1985 Air Chief Marshal Sir David Craig had the honour to name this locomotive ROYAL OBSERVER CORPS at Waterloo Station, pictured here with C/Obs R. Mathews. (C/Obs R. Mathews)

personnel who were not going to be officially introduced to Her Majesty mingled on the lower lawn, upon which a huge white marquee had been erected. Everybody present was entitled to the Royal buffet, which was of a size and magnificence that seemed scarcely conceivable – and for 2,000 guests, as well.

Some observers were selected to line the route of the Royal cars from where they entered the station at the guardroom, to their destination at the Officers' Mess in the Priory. The responsibility for the overall command of these personnel was given to Observer Lieutenant N. B. Creek.

Each group contingent consisted of ten personnel and paraded with other groups of the same area under the command of a nominated officer. The officer in charge of the Southern Area contingent was Observer Officer D. W. Jones; Metropolitan Area was commanded by Observer Lieutenant R. Mitchell; Midland Area by Observer Lieutenant A. R. Whittle; Scottish Area by Observer Lieutenant J. Whittington; and Western Area by Observer Officer J. W. Perrin.

The route from the guardroom to the Priory was lined by a single file of observers. From the guardroom end of this file, the areas paraded in the order of Metropolitan, Midland, Scottish, Southern and Western, with the groups within each area ranged in numerical order. As the Royal cars passed the guardroom and proceeded towards the Priory, the ROC officers saluted, holding the salute until the last car had passed.

Inside the Officers' Mess, the Queen and the Duke of Edinburgh were presented to Air Chief Marshal Sir Thomas Kennedy, Air Chief Marshal Sir David Craig, the Air Officer Commanding-in-Chief of Royal Air Force Strike Command, and Air Commodore Broughton, Commandant of the Royal Observer Corps. Other dignitaries presented to the Queen in the Officers' Mess foyer included Observer Captain S. L. Coffey, Deputy Commandant, Royal Observer Corps; Mr R. F. Cooke, the Director of the United Kingdom Warning and Monitoring Organisation; and Mr W. P. Lawrie and Mr D. L. Warden, Deputy Directors of the UKWMO. In the Rotunda, Her Majesty was introduced to the Assistant Commandant of the Royal Observer Corps, Observer Captain K. Terry, and the five area commandants, Observer Captain D. J. Bridle (Metropolitan Area); Observer Captain W. M. Holmes (Scottish Area); Observer Captain S. G. Deedman (Southern Area); Observer Captain J. G. Brown (Western Area); and Observer Captain J. Shrubbs (Midland Area). A distinguished list of former ROC Commandants included Air Commodore C. M. Wight-Boycott (1961-1964); Air Commodore J. H. Greswell (1964-1968); Air Commodore D. F. Rixson (1968-1970); Air Commodore E. B. Sismore (1971-1973); and Air Vice-Marshal M. H. Miller (1975-1977). Also present were Air Vice-Marshal J. F. G. Howe, Commandant-General RAF Regiment and Director of Security, who was Commandant of the ROC from 1977-1980; Air Vice-Marshal G. P. Black, Deputy Chief of Staff Operations, Allied Air Forces Central Europe, Commandant 1983-1984; and Mr R. A. Falconer, Deputy Commandant 1970-1972. The Danish Luftmelderkorpset (LMK) was represented by Colonel E. P. Sneider.

At three-twenty the Central Band of the Royal Air Force played the National Anthem and the Queen appeared on the balcony of the Priory, accompanied by the Duke of Edinburgh and Air Commodore Broughton. Observers stood to attention and officers saluted for the duration of the anthem, while the ROC banner party honoured Her Majesty from the steps of the Priory. No sooner had the band finished playing than the sky was filled with rumbling as the Battle of Britain

Air Commodore Rixson presenting C/Obs Henderson of Maidstone Group with his BEM 1968-70. Note Seaborne flash.
(© Crown copyright 1993/MOD reproduced with the permission of the Controller of HMSO

Memorial Flight appeared overhead. The flypast consisted of the Lancaster bomber 'City of Lincoln', flanked on either side by Spitfire IIA P7350 and Hurricane IIC LF363. As has been said earlier, P7350 was given approval to change its markings for the Jubilee celebrations to represent EB-Z of 41 Squadron, the aircraft donated to the RAF in 1940 by the Observer Corps, and displayed the embellishments of the original aircraft.

After the flypast the Queen, accompanied by Air Commodore Broughton, made her way on to the lawn to meet the assembled observers, while the Duke set about talking to anybody he liked. Her Majesty was no stranger to Bentley Priory, and indeed, the Priory was no stranger to royalty. In 1849 Queen Victoria and Prince Albert had come there to visit the Dowager Queen Adelaide, the widow of William IV, who had leased the Priory in 1846. In 1944 King George VI, accompanied by Winston Churchill and General Eisenhower, visited the ops room. In 1949 the King returned to Bentley Priory, and the following year Princess Elizabeth made her first visit. In 1958 she returned, attending a dinner celebrating the fortieth anniversary of the forming of the Royal Air Force; by then, of course, she had become Queen Elizabeth II. And on 24 June 1966, as we have already seen, the Queen was again at Bentley Priory, this time in honour of twenty-five years of the corps' assumption of the style and title 'Royal'. On that occasion she was to present the corps with the very same banner which now saluted her from the Priory steps.

The walkabout continued until, after the presentation of the assembled observers and officers, the Royal Party returned to the Officers' Mess Rotunda for tea and further presentations. These were: Observer Commander R. L. Smith, Senior Operations Officer, Headquarters Royal Observer Corps; Observer Commander J. Murphy, Senior Administration Officer, HQ ROC; Observer Commander G. H. Paine, Royal Garden Party Project Officer, HQ ROC; Observer Commander R. D. T. Onions, Deputy Area Commandant, Southern Area; Observer Commander S. R. Morrison, Deputy Area Commandant, Scottish Area; Observer Commander R. G. Smith, Deputy Area Commandant, Metropolitan Area;

Observer Commander N. A. Greig, Deputy Area Commandant, Western Area; and Observer Commander N. Chant, Deputy Area Commandant, Midland Area. At four-thirty the Queen appeared on the balcony of the Dowding Room, where she was presented with a diamond-studded hat-pin in the shape of the beacon-lighter's hand holding a flaming torch. She waved it aloft for all present to see. There was a 'Hats off' for the three cheers, when 2,000 black berets flew skywards. The Queen smiled, waved again and disappeared back into the Officers' Mess. The Royal party departed, and the day drew to a close, leaving all present with their cherished memories of a very special occasion in the history of the Royal Observer Corps. As for the author – he didn't meet the Queen, but he did get to talk to the Duke of Edinburgh.

In April, Air Commodore Broughton had officially opened an exhibition in the West Courtyard of Durham Castle to celebrate the sixtieth anniversary of the Corps. The centre-piece of the exhibition was a 17-foot-long section of fuselage from the Messerschmitt 110 that Rudolf Hess had piloted to Scotland in May 1941. The corps had a particular association with the aircraft, of course, since they had tracked it; apparently, visitors to the Durham ROC centre could see the actual plot displayed in the canteen there.

1985 may well have been the Diamond Jubilee year, a time of great celebration, but it was also a time when the corps was coming under increasing criticism from the Campaign for Nuclear Disarmament (CND). Perhaps it is a trifle naive to say so, but it is difficult to understand this opposition. After all, the job of the ROC was to warn and assist the general public in the event of a nuclear incident. CND, however, appeared to believe that the corps might have an active role in the carrying out of a nuclear attack. One cannot escape the feeling that they had their wires crossed somewhere along the line, but the fact was that they looked upon the Corps with suspicion and fear, as though there were something sinister about the organization.

CND began a campaign at this time of disrupting ROC exercises. Groups of their local CND supporters – men, women and children – would appear at monitoring posts whenever a major exercise was taking place. They tended just to stand about, watching what was going on and asking questions, but it could be quite a daunting experience for observers, trying to carry out their duties while a gang of people waved placards and shouted abuse. Because of the problem, every time there was an exercise the police had to issue each post with a code-word, to be used in the eventuality of subversive activity, as they put it. Code-words like 'Giotto' and 'Pink Alert' would be broadcast to centre, which in turn would contact the police, who would then spring to the observers' aid, like cavalry rushing to help besieged homesteaders in some old western. What was never clear was how CND always knew when there was going to be an exercise in the first place. After all, such information was meant to be restricted. It was probable that the information was obtained through local authorities with so called 'Nuclear Free' policies.

Also at about this time, a campaign of vandalism began in some areas against both group headquarters and monitoring posts. Since the posts were, in many cases, quite remote, they made easy targets for people bent on decorating them with slogans and other graffiti without being disturbed. It is not known who the actual culprits of this vandalism were, since so far as the author is aware they were never caught. The author's own post was daubed with various slogans and symbols on a number of occasions, and one group even tried to break into the post by sawing through the padlocks, though luckily they were not successful.

On 6 June 1985, to mark the forty-first anniversary of D-Day, a special celebration was held in order to allow some of the remaining seaborne observers to return to sea. It had been noticed that HMS *Boxer*, a stretched Type 22 frigate, had the same motto as the Royal Observer Corps – *'Praemonitus Praemunitus'*, a Latin version of 'Forewarned is Forearmed'. Initially it was planned to have a number of ROC personnel visit the ship and present her captain with a plaque. The idea had originated with No 12 Group Bristol, but as preparations got under way, it was decided to invite as many of the remaining 'seabornes' as space would allow. For observers like

The Rt. Hon. Sir Leon Brittan QC
Vice-President of the Commission of the European Communities

During my period in the Home Office I came to
have the highest possible regard for the Royal
Observer Corps, both because of what I knew of
the importance of its work, and because of the
dedication and enthusiasm of its members which
I saw at first hand when visiting the Corps'
camps.

I was particularly impressed by the fact that
the Corps attracted people of all ages and
backgrounds who shared only one thing in
common: their readiness to give freely of
their time in order to be able to help their
country, by gathering information needed to
save lives, if the worst eventuality were ever
to incur. It was a task that was not
glamourous, but most certainly crucial.

I am very glad indeed that the work of the
Royal Observer Corps is now being recorded for
posterity.

Fred Hemenway from No 20 Group York, and Jack McTear from No 1 Group Maidstone, it must have been a very moving experience. *Boxer* was, of course, very different from the ships in which they had sailed in 1944. At 480 feet and with a ship's company of 250, she was as large as many Second World War cruisers. She was armed with both Exocet and Sea Wolf missile systems, though she still employed a pair of 40-mm Bofors guns, which would have been familiar to any wartime observer. After a tour of the ship, the brass plaque (made by Observer Officer Norman Parker) was presented to Lieutenant-Commander Chris Craddock, *Boxer's* First Officer. The Royal Observer Corps received a plaque in return, an exchange that re-established the old link with the Royal Navy, with whom the seaborne observers had served with such dedication and efficiency. In many ways, the ROC plaque, and the corps badge upon it, make a fitting dedication to the Royal Navy. In the days of the Elizabeathan beacon-lighter, it was the navy that largely gained from the beacon fires set ablaze by those early observers. In 1588 the British fleet was forewarned of the approach of the Spanish Armada and spurred into action, in much the same way that a squadron of Spitfires would have been warned at the height of the Battle of Britain.

The Royal Observer Corps training camps since the 1966 Royal Review had been: Coningsby, 1967; Honington, 1968; Watton, 1969 and 1970; West Raynham, 1971; Brawdy, 1972; Lindholme, 1973 and 1974; Colerne, 1975; Little Rissington, 1976; Cosford, 1977, 1978 and 1979; West Raynham again, 1980, 1981 and 1982; and Scampton in 1983 and 1984. The Jubilee camp in 1985 was held at RAF Leeming in North Yorkshire, and for the first time included a first-aid course. It was recognised by now that at least one observer on a post should be trained in the basic principles of first aid. The week's course was instructed by the Fire Officers at RAF Leeming, and led to an exercise during which observers had to rescue casualties from a smoke-filled building, 'damaged' by the (simulated) effects of a bomb blast, and then assess and treat their wounds. The VIP guest who watched the exercise during one of the camps was Leon Brittan, MP, who at that time was the Home Secretary.

Not many months before, on 12 October 1984, he had been present when the Grand Hotel in Brighton, in which many senior delegates to the Conservative Party conference were staying, was bombed by the IRA in an attempt to assassinate Mrs Thatcher and the rest of her Cabinet. The scenes that the poor man had to witness during the corps' little play must have brought back some terrifying memories for him.

As a symbolic celebration for the Diamond Jubilee it was decided to hold a run, beginning at the Lizard in Cornwall and ending at Royal Observer Corps Headquarters at Bentley Priory. The run was a relay, and took place on the weekend of the 26/28 July, a torch bearing a message from the Commandant of No 10 Group Exeter eventually being handed to Air Commodore Broughton, the Corps Commandant. But, for a number of reasons, the run almost did not go ahead. No 9 Group Yeovil became the victim of unforeseen complications when the police decided that it was far too dangerous for people to run along the busy A30 London to Penzance road on a summer weekend. Eventually, group headquarters at Yeovil and the police together came up with a plan to save the day. It was decided that all the runners for that particular section would congregate on a quiet stretch of road just outside Yeovil, and that each person would cover their distance of 3.6 miles over the same ground, until the required total had been achieved. So in the end the run was not a complete relay, but torch and message did get to reach their final destination. The message contained within the torch read:

To the Commandant, Royal Observer Corps, Greetings, in this Diamond Jubilee year of 1985, from the southernmost point of your Command. Let both this message and its means of conveyance symbolise the principle of communicating the warning of danger to our Nation. From the Lizard Post in Cornwall, to Headquarters Bentley Priory near London, this means of conveying communication has been made possible by the co-operative joining together of elements of our warning chain. Since the days of the Elizabeth I Beacon-Lighter, depicted in our emblem, to the present day in the reign of Elizabeth II, our Air Commodore-in-Chief, the message remains, Forewarned is Forearmed. G. J. Shrimpton, Commandant No 10 Group ROC.

In 1984, the Queen had honoured Observer Commander Shrimpton by appointing him MBE. He had had a distinguished career with the corps, having joined as a post observer in 1955, in what was then 11 Group. After promotion to leading observer, he became an observer officer in March 1963, and in 1978 was presented with the Lord Lieutenant's Certificate of Meritorious Service. He was promoted to observer lieutenant in May 1980 and to observer commander on 1 August 1982, when he took up his appointment as Group Commandant of No 10 Group Exeter. He also had a very busy civilian life, being head of the Mining Department at Camborne School of Mines, and Director of the BSc Mining Degree Course which is run annually at the school. He was also the Honorary Curator of the Royal Geological Society Museum, and in 1976 was presented with the William Bolitho Gold Medal of the Royal Geological Society.

Many groups held their own celebrations for the Diamond Jubilee. Amongst the most impressive was a service of thanksgiving held on 29 September in Lincoln Cathedral by No 15 Group Lincoln. The guests included the Lord Lieutenant of Lincolnshire and his wife, the Mayor and Sheriff of the City of Lincoln, and the station commanders of Royal Air Forces Scampton, Waddington, Swinderby and Coningsby. The attendance of these and other distinguished guests helped to give the corps a high public profile towards the end of its special year. For the service at Lincoln the Royal Observer Corps Banner was allowed out of Bentley Priory. Observer Lieutenant Geoff Whitworth had the privilege of being the Banner bearer, and the escort were Chief Observer T. Hancock, Leading Observer K. Slater and Leading Observer D. Cowley.

No 9 Group Yeovil held a service of thanksgiving at Wells Cathedral on Saturday 9 November, which coincided with Remembrance weekend. The lessons were read by Chief Observer S. P. Smordon from group headquarters and Woman Observer S. M. Luxton from Sidmouth Post, and the ushers were Observer Lieutenant I. A. Woodley and Observer Officer

J. W. G. Norman. The theme of the thanksgiving service was the work of the Royal Observer Corps, in particular its accomplishments during the Second World War.

Taking part in the annual Festival of Remembrance at the Royal Albert Hall had become one of the corps' annual public performances. For the Diamond Jubilee it was fitting that the corps' representatives were selected from members of the oldest group, which was, of course, No 1 Group Maidstone. It is interesting to note that the contingents which take part in the festival do not merely turn up on the day and march into the hall – a great deal of preparation has to go into the event. The observers from Maidstone had to undergo three days of training at RAF Uxbridge under NCOs of the Queen's Colour Squadron, Royal Air Force Regiment. Particular attention was given to the problem of marching down the steps, and even on the day itself there were dress rehearsals at the Albert Hall before the final parade in front of Her Majesty the Queen. The Royal Observer Corps' long and close association with the RAF is always made evident at the parade. The ROC contingent is always introduced with the reserve branches of the RAF, such as the Royal Auxiliary Air Force, and as such would parade with them and not the civilian organizations which followed.

On 6 December 1985 the Commandant, Air Commodore Broughton, and the Deputy Commandant, Observer Captain Coffey, visited the Bomber Command Museum and made a formal presentation of a cheque for £3,250 to the museum. The Commandant also presented the museum with a mounted bomb fragment. In 1975, No 14 Group Winchester had recovered and reconstructed a 'dambuster'-type bomb, and presented it to No 617 Squadron RAF, the Dambuster Squadron. During the reclamation of that bomb, large pieces of another were also recovered. With the exception of one large piece of this second bomb (which was later presented to the Warnham War Museum at Horsham), the spare pieces remained at Winchester Group. Eventually it was decided to cut the pieces into small fragments, about an inch square, and mount them on shields like the ones that carry RAF squadron crests, the idea being to sell them as a limited edition in order to raise money for the Bomber Command Museum. In the end, the metal was cut up by RAF apprentices and mounted on wooden blocks, crests having proved far too expensive. The museum was to use the donation to aid the setting up of a tribute to Marshal of the RAF Sir Arthur 'Bomber' Harris, C-in-C of Bomber Command from 1942-1945. A reconstructed mine guards the gate at RAF Scampton, and the inscription on it reads: 'The Barnes Wallis Mine was reconstructed by No 14 Group Royal Observer Corps, from casing recovered from Fordingbridge bombing range and presented to No 617 Squadron. It was unveiled in October 1975 by members of the squadron who flew on the raid which breached the Möhne and Eder Dams.'

1985 was without doubt one of the busiest, most memorable, and perhaps most controversial years in the history of the Royal Observer Corps. When it is considered that the corps had so few years of service left, the celebrations which took place throughout 1985 acted as a lasting and worthy tribute.

Above: The ROC contingent who took part in the Battle of Britain Parade in September 1990 at Buckingham Palace, pose at Wellington Barracks. Taking part, although not in this order on the photograph are: A. Bradshaw, L. Burt, C. Jerrold, R. Rowe, J. McClay, E. Allison, P. Stone, P. Shire, M. Allison, A. Griffiths, M. Whitcher, C. Shire, R. Blackwell, G. Senior, D. Beale, J. Searle, K. Burma, M. Bevan, T. Gay, A. Smith, J. Towner, F. Stone, P. Blackwell, D. Green, R. Cullingford, B. Griffiths, C. John, E. Spicer, S. Moore, B. Scott, D. Cowley. (ROCM/C/Obs (W) Rita Cullingford)

Below: Members of the ROC museum team at the re-opening of the museum in Winchester in October 1987. From left to right: Ian Joslin, Phil Mulvey, Rita Cullingford, Neville Cullingford and Mike Merritt. (ROCM/Obs Lt N. Cullingford)

CHAPTER ELEVEN
Royal Review

In September 1986 Air Commodore I. Horrocks replaced Air Commodore Broughton as Commandant of the Royal Observer Corps. Air Commodore Broughton was, however, to remain with the corps just long enough for a minor upset to rock the steadfast morale of observers young and old. Every summer since 1948, when the first training camp had been held at Thorney Island, the Royal Air Force had provided a venue worthy of the relationship between the two organizations. In 1986, when it was announced that the camp would be held at the University of Newcastle-upon-Tyne, there were rumblings of dissatisfaction. And nobody knows this better than the author who, as one of the younger observers present, had to sit and listen to the older members moaning during meal breaks. This in itself upset them, as they had always been used to 'the mess' and 'NAAFI breaks'. As it turned out the camp had more of a military feel than most. While the ROC were there a big military show was being held nearby and many of the participants were also being accommodated on the campus, and would mingle with observers in the residence halls, dining halls and student bars.

In 1987 things happily returned to normal, as the camp was held at RAF Waddington. Newcastle turned out to be a one-off blemish on an otherwise spotless catalogue of names. The remaining few camps were held at Waddington in 1988, Watton in 1989, and the very last camp returned to Watton in 1990.

1991 was destined to be a very special year long before anybody was even remotely aware that the corps' vital role within the UKWMO was to be wound down. It was, of course, the fiftieth anniversary of the Observer Corps' assumption of the style and title 'Royal'. A Royal Review at Bentley Priory was planned for 25 July, only a few months before the corps was officially stood down. This, then, was to be their finest

The Rt. Hon. Lord Ferrers

HOME OFFICE

The Home Office greatly valued the magnificent contribution which the professional and dedicated volunteers of the Royal Observer Corps made to the work of the Home Office Warning and Monitoring system.

We deeply appreciated the enthusiasm and the efficiency with which they always carried out their operational task. Over 66 years they gave devoted and loyal service to the Corps and to the country, and we are indebted to them.

Yours sincerely,

Ferrers.

celebration.

Air Commodore G. M. Boddy had taken over from Air Commodore I. Horrocks in September 1989, to become the Commandant who would see the corps through the final years of its then status.

Buckingham Palace had announced in January 1991 the intention to hold a Royal Review and Garden Party, at which both Her Majesty the Queen and His Royal Highness the Duke of Edinburgh would be present. Preparations for the event were to involve an incredible number of different organisations. A planning committee headed by the Chief of Staff, Observer Captain Murphy, handled the complex issues which had to be covered. A new Banner was even commissioned, as the one which Her Majesty had presented to the corps in 1966 was showing signs of age. Wing-Commander Peter Storey, P1 (Ceremonials) RAF, gave advice on protocol. There was to be a parade involving 2,000 observers and officers, and the Queen's Colour Squadron of the RAF Regiment had the unenviable task of translating the broad parade outline into reality. The Banner Party and Escort Flight had to attend RAF Uxbridge for drill instruction from the Queen's Colour Squadron.

On the day of the Review security around Bentley Priory was once again extremely tight. A helicopter buzzed overhead, while numerous mounted civilian policemen patrolled the surrounding area. Basically, the RAF police were responsible for security within the Priory grounds and the civilian police outside. As with the Diamond Jubilee celebration, the Irish and Scottish contingents were specially flown down, most of the other groups arriving by coach.

The parade formed up at one-thirty and at two-fifteen the reception party assembled, ready for the arrival of the Royal cars at two-twenty-five. On arriving at Bentley Priory Her Majesty the Queen and His Royal Highness the Duke of Edinburgh were received by Archie Hamilton, the Armed Forces Minister, who then presented Lord Ferrers, Home Office Minister, the Mayor and Mayoress of Harrow, Air Chief Marshal Sir Peter Harding, Air Vice-Marshal Sir William Wrattan, and Air Commodore Boddy. A few minutes later, the

The Rt. Hon. Archie Hamilton MP
Minister of State for the Armed Forces

MINISTRY OF DEFENCE

The Royal Observer Corps has played a vital
part in our defence effort, notably during the
Second World War, and also thereafter, when
its role broadened into nuclear warning and
monitoring.

Those who belonged to the Royal Observer Corps
can be justifiably proud of having given such
excellent and dedicated service over many
decades.

You sincerely
Archie Hamilton

144

Royal party was escorted on foot to the parade ground dais, and at about the same time the Battle of Britain Memorial Flight passed overhead in salute. The Review itself followed, the Royal couple, accompanied by Air Commodore Boddy and Observer Captain John Murphy (the Review Commander), inspecting the parade from the comfort of an open-topped vehicle.

Throughout the Review music was provided by the Central Band of the RAF under its Principal Director of Music, Wing-Commander H. B. Hingley. While the old Banner was marched past Her Majesty, the Central Band played 'Skywatch', the official march of the Royal Observer Corps. It had been composed in 1975 by Wing-Commander R. E. C. Davies, to celebrate the fiftieth anniversary of the founding of the Corps. Wing-Commander Davies was at the time the Organizing Director of Music for the RAF, and the Queen had graciously granted approval for the march to be used by the corps.

After the old Banner had been marched past, the new Banner was consecrated by the Chaplain-in-Chief of the Royal Air

Air Commodore Orrock presents Wing Commander Roy Davies, the composer of Skywatch, with a commemorative plate in the concert hall of RAF Music Services, Uxbridge, in 1975. (Wing Commander Davies)

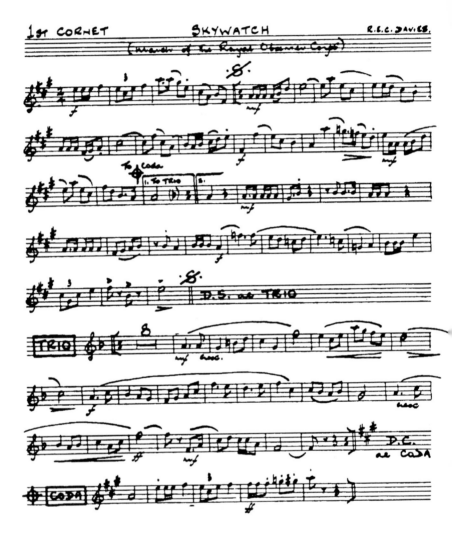

Skywatch, the march of the Royal Observer Corps was composed by Wing Commander Roy E C Davies, to commemorate the Golden Jubilee of the Corps in 1975. This copy of the 1st cornet part has been provided by Wing Commander H B Hingley, Principal Director of Music, The Royal Air Forces Music Services. Reproduced with the permission of Boosey & Hawkes Music Publishers Ltd.

Force, the Venerable B. N. Halfpenny. The Banner Bearer, Observer Lieutenant Terry Giles, knelt before the Queen, who presented the new Banner, with some assistance from the Commandant. Following the presentation, Her Majesty was invited to address the parade. A copy of her speech has been kindly provided for publication by Sir Kenneth Scott, Her Majesty's Private Secretary at Buckingham Palace, and appears at the beginning of this book.

After the Queen's address, the Commandant replied on behalf of the corps.

Your Majesty. Before you are 2,000 of your Observers. They represent every element of the Corps and accurately reflect our nationwide membership. Only once before – in 1945 – has so large a parade been held, when the Royal Air Force expressed its gratitude for the Corps' support during the war. That occasion too foreshadowed a stand-down of the Corps because, as now, we had completed the work we had been asked to do. So today we do have mixed feelings, but we are privileged and especially heartened by being able to appear, in Review, before you – our Air Commodore-in-Chief. We are grateful also for this opportunity to commemorate and celebrate key events in the proud history of a unique Corps. A Corps in which many thousands of your subjects from all parts of the nation and from many different backgrounds have freely given service. Their loyalty to you, to our country, has been absolute and will continue. Less than a quarter of the Corps is actually present in Review but I know that the pride shown by those here today is felt equally strongly by all Observers and that they too share in our expression of loyalty. Your gracious presentation of a new Banner will provide us with a fitting reminder of the faithful service of the Corps over many years and of your Royal patronage. Your Majesty, your Royal Observer Corps thanks you.

At three o'clock the Queen and the Duke of Edinburgh visited the Officers' Mess, where they were greeted by the President of the Mess Committee, Wing-Commander David Roome. Also presented were Observer Captain and Mrs

Murphy, Observer Captains Gerald Brown and Joyce Shrubbs (the Assistant Commandants), and the Commandant's wife, Mrs Boddy.

To mark the special day, Her Majesty was presented with an engraved Caithness Glass bowl which, among other things, depicted observers at the time of the Battle of Britain and the seaborne adventure. The bowl had been specially made for the corps by master glassblower Franco Toffolo, and had been designed and engraved by Helen MacDonald. Its inscription read: 'Presented to Her Majesty Queen Elizabeth II, Air Commodore-in-Chief, Royal Observer Corps, on the occasion of The Royal Review at Bentley Priory and in celebration of the Fiftieth Anniversary of the style and title 'Royal' 25th July 1991.'

Whilst in the Ladies' Ante-Room in the Officers' Mess, the Queen was to see, in its new home there, a portrait of her that had been specially commissioned for the occasion. To greet her were the artist Mara McGregor and Wing-Commander McGregor. All twenty-five ROC groups had contributed to the cost of the portrait and, after six sittings, a quite remarkable likeness was achieved by the artist. Mara McGregor's other works had included a portrait of HRH The Prince of Wales, and two portraits of Her Majesty Queen Elizabeth the Queen Mother, one of which hangs in the Rotunda of the Bentley Priory Officers' Mess.

Her Majesty next met the five Area Commandants: Observer Captain Gordon Martin (Scottish Area); Observer Captain Brian McCarthy (Metropolitan Area); Observer Captain Michael Marks (Midland Area); Observer Captain Alan Price-Talbot (Southern Area); and Observer Captain Harold Archer (Western Area). The new Banner was then attended by Observer Lieutenant Giles and inspected by Her Majesty.

Following tea with the senior guests, the Queen was accompanied into the garden by the Commandant, while, on the balcony of the Officers' Mess, trumpeters of the Central Band of the RAF heralded her arrival. Her Majesty and the Duke of Edinburgh were then introduced to many of the guests who had assembled in the Priory gardens.

After the Garden Party, the Royal couple retired to the

Officers' Mess, where they signed the Banner and Visitors' Books, and at four-twenty-five the Banner Party led the Royal Salute. The Banner Escort consisted of Chief Observer K. Budd from No 2 Group Horsham, Leading Observer R. S. Hind from No 13 Group South Wales, and Leading Observer J. F. Keeping from No 16 Group Shrewsbury.

The new Banner was lowered for the Salute, while the Royal party watched from the balcony of the Main Ante-Room, and there followed the customary and rousing three cheers with black berets off. Then, at four-thirty, the Queen and the Duke of Edinburgh left the Priory for Buckingham Palace.

14 Group personnel in front of Chinook of 7 Squadron during final ROC flight from RAF Odiham 23 September 1991. Standing left to right: C/Obs K. Holdsworth, Obs G. Dumas, Obs S. Palmer, Obs D. Rolls, Obs C. Dunn, Obs T. Gowers, Obs (W) P. Bridger, C/Obs C. King, Obs M. Merritt, C/Obs (W) L. Oliver, Obs (W) W. Burch, Obs (W) J. Atyeo, Obs (W) R. King, Obs C. Smith, C/Obs J. Pritchard, Obs (W) M. Preselo, Obs G. Baxter. Kneeling: Obs J. Hards, C/Obs A. Hackwell, Obs Lt N. Cullingford, L/Obs S. Doel. (© Crown copyright 1993/MOD reproduced with the permission of the Controller of HMSO)

On the penultimate day of the Royal Observer Corps' service, Sunday 29 September 1991, a service was held at St Clement Danes in London, the Central Church of the Royal Air Force. The service, which was attended by 320 officers and observers from every group of the corps, witnessed the laying-up of the Sovereign's Banner of the Royal Observer Corps, which had been presented in 1966. Officiating during the laying-up ceremony was the resident chaplain, Padre Tom Goode, and also present was ex-Observer Commander Derrick Ballington, who had been the Banner Bearer when it was first presented to the corps in 1966. As the Banner Party entered the church they were accompanied by the pealing of the bells, and their route was lined by observers from No 2 Group Horsham. There followed a fanfare by the trumpeters of the Central Band, RAF, while the Banner was marched in slow time past the congregation to the altar steps. The last officer to salute the passing Banner was Observer Lieutenant-Commander G. I. Hartley. Air Commodore Boddy, in handing over the Sovereign's Banner, said: 'Reverend Sir, I ask you to receive this Banner of the Royal Observer Corps for safe keeping in the House of God.' The Banner now hangs alongside the many other banners, colours, standards and ensigns of the Royal Air Force in the church.

On the following day, 30 September, the vast majority of corps members were officially stood down. In his final farewell message, the Chief of Staff, Observer Captain John Murphy, who was subsequently awarded the OBE in the Queen's 1992 Birthday Honours List, said:

Well, what of the future? Many of you will find ways of expressing your volunteer spirit and invest your spare time in other community based organisations, but your service in the Royal Observer Corps will never be forgotten. The corps was stood down before and that proved not to be the end. Who can predict with any certainty the pattern of future events and the subsequent need for an organization such as ours? Might we one day be required to stand-to again?

The Commandant's farewell message included the following passage:

The reality and inevitability of stand-down has now been driven home as we recover and hand back equipment. You must, however, take consolation from the fact that we are not being disbanded and that our Nuclear Reporting Cells will for the moment continue. Thus a spark at least of the corps ethos will remain and it must be preserved until the country is able to determine its long-term need for volunteer forces. That might not be until the middle of this decade. Meanwhile we must stay in contact, preferably through the medium of the ROC Association. I want to make particular mention here of your families, for no observer could have given the commitment so much in evidence everywhere without the wholehearted support of his or her family. The families too are part of the corps' unique social community. I thank you all for the exceptional service you have so freely given and I wish you all good fortune for the future.

Many organizations would quite easily have fallen apart at the seams after receiving such devastating news. In typical style, the members of the Royal Observer Corps stayed loyal and enthusiastic to the end. In a letter to the author, the Southern Area Commandant, Observer Captain Alan Price-Talbot, sums up the corps' spirit in those last few moments.

Despite the intense disappointment and disbelief felt by all ranks, which many outside the Corps thought would lead to the immediate disintegration of the organisation, the Corps worked hard during those last few months dismantling and delivering post equipment to collection meetings. Stripping and removing operational items from controls and generally carrying on as a uniformed and disciplined body. It is a cause of great pride to all senior officers that the Corps Stood Down in such good order. I will never forget the last night Sept. 30th. The Commandant joined us in Truro for a last combined cluster and afterwards as midnight approached, champagne was provided and we marked the end of an era in some style. But unplanned and without order at one minute past the hour all the spare-time officers who were then effectively Stood-Down, removed their rank sleeves

The Rt. Hon. TOM KING, C.H., M.P.

HOUSE OF COMMONS

My time as Secretary of State for Defence witnessed the momentous changes in Eastern Europe and the collapse of the former Soviet Union that brought the Cold War to a close. With these changes came the ending of the Corps' role as the field force of the United Kingdom Warning and Monitoring Organisation and the stand down of the Corps for the second time in its history. While the Corps was operationally responsible to UKWMO and therefore to the Home Secretary in this role, it was clear to me that the close association between the Royal Observer Corps and the Royal Air Force forged during World War II and continuing through the years of the Cold War was of great importance to both Services.

Tl.e record of service and the voluntary contribution which members of the Corps have made over the past sixty years has been outstanding.

from their shirt epaulettes. The Commandant was visibly moved, because it was done voluntarily, responsibly and without rancour and that sums it up.

As the Royal Observer Corps stood down in September 1991, for the second time in its history, 250 members were retained under the auspices of RAF Strike Command. Stand-down is, of course, far from being the end. Through the medium of the newly formed Royal Observer Corps Association, which is based on the former group identities, the spirit of comradeship and good fellowship will be preserved. In 1992, under the leadership of Joyce Shrubbs, 200 members of ROCA took part in the Armistice Day Parade at the Cenotaph in Whitehall and proudly marched past into Horse Guards, where His Royal Highness Prince Andrew took the salute. ROCA will also allow former members to keep in touch should their services be required in the future. The Association also provides close support for, and vital links with, the ROC Benevolent Fund, which gives assistance to former members and their families who may have fallen on hard times. As can be seen, the history continues.

There were, presumably, a number of reasons for the decision to stand down the Corps. In a letter to the author dated June 1992, the Home Secretary at the time, Kenneth Baker stated that local authorities now have their own civil defence radiation monitoring. The then Secretary of State for Defence, Tom King, explained that the decision was governed largely by the collapse of the former Soviet Union and the ending of the Cold War. There was also, inevitably, a financial aspect to the decision. But at least a small element of the corps remains. And at least its

The Rt. Hon. Tom King MP. (Bridgwater Constituency Conservative Association)

The Rt. Hon. KENNETH BAKER, M.P.

HOUSE OF COMMONS

The Royal Observer Corps was formed in 1925 originally to spot incoming enemy aircraft. Over the years, the Corps' role expanded into warning and monitoring air attacks, the fall and yield of nuclear bombs and the levels of radioactive fall-out. This has been a vital responsibility. The ROC has done a magnificent job for the Home Office. As Home Secretary at the time, I regretted having to make the decision to stand down the Corps but it was unavoidable as local authorities have now developed their own civil defence radiation monitoring.

I remain deeply grateful to the Royal Observer Corps for the dedication and professionalism which they have shown over 66 years of loyal service. I hope that the enthusiasm and skills of the ROC's volunteers are not lost either to civil defence or to other volunteer organisations.

identity and association with the Royal Air Force will be maintained and, it is hoped, carried far into the future. To further cement this link, when Air Commodore Boddy retired in May 1992, the new Commandant, Air Commodore M. P. Donaldson, was also at that time the Senior Air Staff Officer No 11 Group RAF

All the observers whom the author has had the pleasure to know have had one thing in common – the Royal Observer Corps remains a part of their present as well as their past. They remember with pride their years of service, and fondly cherish the unique sense of humour that went with the uniform. The corps will be sadly missed by all. But the memories and bonds which it forged will keep its spirit firmly in the present, safe in the knowledge that if the country should ever need it again, there will be a mad rush of volunteers ready to serve.

The following passage is taken from *The Armada*, a long narrative poem written in 1842 by Thomas Babington, Lord Macaulay (1800-1859), the historian, essayist and politician. It is used here as a final tribute to the spirit and principle of the Royal Observer Corps. Like the beacon-lighters of 1588, the men and women of the corps were always ready to spread the warning. Even through the darkest hours of Britain's history, the message remained 'Forewarned is Forearmed.'

Night sank upon the dusky beach, and on the purple sea,
Such night in England ne'er had been, nor e'er again shall be.
From Eddystone to Berwick bounds, from Lynn to Milford Bay,
That time of slumber was as bright and busy as the day;
For swift to east and swift to west the ghastly war-flame spread.
High on St Michael's Mount it shone: it shone on Beachy Head.
Far on the deep the Spaniard saw, along each southern shire,
Cape beyond cape, in endless range, those twinkling points of fire.
The fisher left his skiff to rock on Tamar's glittering waves:
The rugged miners poured to war from Mendip's sunless caves:
O'er Longleat's towers, o'er Cranbourne's oaks, the fiery herald flew:
He roused the shepherds of Stonehenge, the rangers of

Beaulieu.

Right sharp and quick the bells all night rang out from Bristol town,
And ere the day three hundred horse had met on Clifton Down;
The sentinel on Whitehall gate looked forth into the night,
And saw o'erhanging Richmond Hill the streak of blood-red light.
Then bugle's note and cannon's roar the deathlike silence broke,
And with one start, and with one cry, the royal city woke.
At once on all her stately gates arose the answering fires;
At once the wild alarum clashed from all her reeling spires;
From all the batteries of the Tower pealed loud the voice of fear;
And all the thousand masts of Thames sent back a louder cheer:
And from the furthest wards was heard the rush of hurrying feet,
And the broad streams of pikes and flags rushed down each roaring street;
And broader still became the blaze, and louder still the din,
As fast from every village round the horse came spurring in:
And eastward straight from wild Blackheath the warlike errand went,
And roused in many an ancient hall the gallant squires of Kent.
Southward from Surrey's pleasant hills flew those bright couriers forth;
High on bleak Hampstead's swarthy moor they started for the north;
And on, and on, without a pause, untired they bounded still:
All night from tower to tower they sprang; they sprang from hill to hill:
Till the proud peak unfurled the flag o'er Darwin's rocky dales,
Till like volcanoes flared to heaven the stormy hills of Wales,
Till twelve fair counties saw the blaze on Malvern's lonely height,
Till streamed in crimson on the wind the Wrekin's crest of light,
Till broad and fierce the star came forth on Ely's stately fane,
And tower and hamlet rose in arms o'er all the boundless plain;
Till Belvoir's lordly terraces the sign to Lincoln sent,

And Lincoln sped the message on o'er the wide vale of Trent;
Till Skiddaw saw the fire that burned on Gaunt's embattled
pile,
And the red glare on Skiddaw roused the burghers of Carlisle.

The Rt. Hon. Paddy Ashdown MP.
(Paddy Ashdown)

The Rt. Hon Douglas Hurd MP.
(Foreign & Commonwealth Office)

The Rt. Hon. Michael Heseltine MP.
(Department of Trade & Industry)

Margaret, The Lady Thatcher OM
PC FRC (Lady Thatcher's Private
Office)

The Rt. Hon. Paddy Ashdown MP

HOUSE OF COMMONS

The Royal Observer Corps has for many years, including amongst them some of the darkest moments of Britain's history, acted as front line of defence for our country. I had the privilege on one occasion of visiting the Royal Observer Corps Headquarters in Southwoods in Yeovil. There I met some excellent citizens from Yeovil and its district, who gave up their time to make sure that our population was a little safer.

The Royal Observer Corps is now, regrettably, part of Britain's history. But it is I fancy a history that will not easily be forgotten by those who understood the importance of the Corps at moments of National Danger.

The Rt. Hon. Michael Heseltine MP

HOUSE OF COMMONS

I am as aware as anyone who lived through the dark days of World War Two of the magnificent contribution of the Royal Observer Corps to our national defences. As a nation we owe an incalculable debt of gratitude to those who served as the eyes and the ears of the country in the front line of the home defence. And during the uncertainty of the Cold War years that followed the Corps continued to play a critical role.

If, as a result of the momentous changes in international politics in the last few years, that role is no longer necessary, we will never forget what we owe to all those who served so selflessly and bravely throughout years of devoted service.

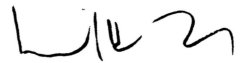

Foreign &
Commonwealth Office

I am delighted to be able to be given this
opportunity to express my admiration for the
work of the Royal Observer Corps. It gave me
great pleasure, as Home Secretary, to inspect
the Corps' Annual Parade, and I have
particularly fond memories of my visits to its
headquarters. Each of those occasions brought
home to me the outstanding contribution which
the Corps has made to the safety of our
country.

The Corps was a remarkable embodiment of the
voluntary spirit from which Britain draws so
much strength. Its place in history is
guaranteed.

Douglas Hurd.

The Rt. Hon. Baroness Thatcher OM FRS

I will remember the importance of the Royal
Observer Corps during the darkest days of the
War. Their service to our country and people
was an example of all that is best in the
British character - invincible and
indomitable. I am grateful to have the chance
to pay tribute to each and every one of those
who served.

Margaret Thatcher

Air Commodore M.A. Harvey RAF (Retd)

It was inevitable, perhaps, in a world of
increasing dependence on high technology,
changing political relationships and severe
financial stringency, that a future role for
the Royal Observer Corps could not easily be
found. This is a pity, for over many years the
ROC has proved itself extremely versatile and
flexible, adapting itself to new tasks and
wider horizons with commendable speed and
skill. Furthermore, it provided an invaluable
interface between the RAF and the civilian
population, as well as a companionable
brotherhood for those with the interests of
the Service at heart. The dedication of its
members over 66 years will be greatly missed.

Yours sincerely

Maurice Harvey

The Rt. Hon. Lord Carrington

I remember very well in the days of the Second
World War how much we depended upon the Royal
Observer Corps and, incidentally, how greatly
I admired their ability to tell one type of
aircraft from another. I never managed the
difference between a hurricane and a spitfire!

They were an invaluable part of our defence in
those long six years and subsequently gave up
much of their time through acting as a
deterrent against a repetition of the Second
World War. Those of us who fought in that war
are deeply grateful for all they did. They
should be proud of their sixty-six years
service.

The Rt. Hon. Malcolm Rifkind MP
The Secretary of State

MINISTRY OF DEFENCE

Although the Royal Observer Corps was stood
down before I became Secretary of State for
Defence, I am very much aware of the
tremendous contribution that the Corps made
during and since the Second World War, and the
closeness of its association with the RAF.

I greatly welcome this opportunity to pay
tribute to the men and women of the Royal
Observer Corps, who performed such admirable
service for their country.

The Rt. Hon. Lord Jenkins of Hillhead

HOUSE OF LORDS

The Royal Observer Corps performed 66 years of invaluable national service. The Corps was responsible for its operational efficiency, in some ways surprisingly, to the Home Office, and I was the only person who, during those 66 years, was twice Home Secretary. I can therefore speak from the perspective of a span of more than a decade in paying tribute to their quality and performance.

Observer Lieutenant Neville Cullingford

As Curator of the ROC Museum, Winchester, and a member of the Royal Observer Corps for 35 years I wish to pay tribute to the many thousands of my colleagues who have given of their time freely and unselfishly in the ROC for the public good. They have done so with such a fine spirit, and have brought to the art of monitoring, reporting and plotting, an enthusiasm and professionalism which many full-time organisations would envy.In future I will be unable to pass an abandoned ROC post without thinking of the dedicated team of enthusiasts who manned it for 30 odd years; of the puttering battery generator; of the background chatter on the teletalk, of the semi-gloom below which slowly gave way to reveal the warmly-clad crew. Although more comfortable than the posts, the Controls required teamwork, knowledge and alertness of a very high order combined with a heavy workload cheerfully undertaken. All these things and more I will remember, but above all I will remember those close knit teams who manned these lonely out-posts in all weathers and their operations room colleagues who waited patiently for their reports, from which their warnings were issued. The comradeship, loyalty, laughter, keenness, discomfort and even some boredom, shared by its members who came together from all walks of life to work together so democratically, is so very worthy of this Tribute which I am so proud to be able to make.

Neville Cullingford

Index

Biggin Hill 32, 33
Binbrook 105
Birmingham 47
Black, Air Cdr G. 116, 117, 130
Black Thursday 45
Blackwell, P. 140
Blackwell, R. 140
Blenheim (Bristol) 41, 43, 63, 133
Bleriot, Louis 65
Blue Triangle Club 13
Boadicea, Queen 16, 17
Boddy, Air Cdr G. 143, 145, 150, 155
Boddy, Mrs 148
Bodhill, T. H. 72
Boers 7
Bolland, P. 47
Bomber Command 109
Bomb Power Indicator (BPI) 121, 123
Bonaparte, Napoleon 4, 65
Bourne, G. A. D. 72
Bowyer, J. 47
Box 32
Boyd Committee 14
Boyle, Sir Dermott 102
Bradshaw, A. 140
Brand, Air Vice-Marshal Sir Quintin 32
Bratton post 84
Brawdy 135
Bridger, P. 149
Bridle, D. 130
Brittan, Sir Leon 134, 135
Bristol 95, 124
Brize Norton 47
Bromley 79
Brooke, Sir William 2
Broughton, Air Cdre J. 107, 117, 118, 127, 129, 130, 131, 132, 135, 138, 141
Brown, G. 148
Brown J. 130
Brown, W. 108
Brunswick Tower post 90
Buckingham Palace 77, 140, 143, 147, 149
Buckinghamshire 13

Buckton, Henry 107
Budd, K. 149
Bulpett, H. 86
Bulpett, J. 86
Bulson, H. 60
bum-boats 70
Burch, W. 149
Burma, K. 140
Burt, L. 140
Bury St Edmunds 91
Bushnel, G. 47
Butler, R. 101
Cable, K. 82
Callaghan, Rt. Hon. Lord 58, 59
Cambridge 91
Campaign for Nuclear Disarmament (CND) 132
Capitoline Geese 64
Cardiff 91
Carlisle 97, 124
Carrington, Rt. Hon. Lord 163
Castle Bromwich 47
Castletown 33
Catterick 33
Cavotti, Lieutenant 8
Cenotaph 153
Central Band of the RAF 105, 130, 145, 148, 150
Central School of Aircraft Recognition 67
Chain Home 31, 63
Chamberlain, Neville 24, 37
Chant, N. 132
Chapman, A. 60
Charles, His Royal Highness Prince 116, 148
Chasquis 1
Cheshire 23
Chinook 149
Church Fenton 32, 33
Churchill, Winston 37, 45, 50, 65, 74, 81, 131
Clelford, E. 86
Clifton, E. 89
Coastal Command 57
Coastguard Service 57

Heading, P. 72
Heath Robinson 13
Hebrides 97
Heinkel He111 41, 43, 81
Hememway, F. 135
Hendon 33
Henlow 47
Henry VIII, King 17
Hercules 116
Hertfordshire 13
Heseltine, Rt. Hon. Michael MP 158, 160
Hess, Rudolf 54, 132
High Wycombe 109, 111, 126
Hill, Air Marshal Roderic 74, 79, 83, 85
Hind (Hawker) 15
Hind, R. 149
Hingley, Wing-Commander H. 146
Hitler 28, 40, 44, 54, 74, 78, 83, 90
Hoare, P. 47
Hobeliers 3, 4
Holdaway, J. 86
Holdsworth, K. 149
Holland 40, 81
Holmes, W. 130
Home Office 38, 117, 134, 142, 143, 154
Honington 108, 135
Hornchurch 32, 33, 46
Horne, M. 86
Horrocks, Air Cdre I. 141, 143, 145
Horsham 6, 12, 13, 74, 79, 80, 92, 96, 115, 124, 138, 149, 150
Horsham St Faith 105
Hounsome, G. 117
Hounsome, P. 82, 108
Howe, Captain C. L. 57
Howe, Air Cdre J. 113, 114, 130
Hughes, J. 72
Hull 8
Huntley, L/Obs 94
Hurd, Rt. Hon. Douglas MP 158, 161
Hurricane (Hawker) 28, 41, 43, 44, 63, 131, 163
Hyde, C. 86

Hyde, F. 60
Hyde, S. 60
Iceni 16, 17
Incas 2
Ingham 9
Inverness 97, 109, 111, 124
Isaiah 1
Isle of Man 97
Isle of Wight 32
Italy 8
Jackson, J. 108
James, D. 72
Jeffery, E. 101, 108
Jenkins, Rt. Hon. Lord 165
Jeremiah 1
Jerrold, C. 140
Jewell, C/Obs S. 75
John, C. 140
Johnson, Air Vice-Marshal J. E. 48, 49, 50
Jones, D. 129
Jones, E. 72
Jones, M. 60
Jordan, Air Cdre R. 87
Joslin, I. 140
Joubert de la Ferte, Air Marshal Philip 53
Junkers Ju87B 41, 42
Junkers Ju88A 41, 43
Juno Beach 71
Keeping, J. 149
Keeping, M. 108
Kelly, B. 82
Kempster, L/Obs G. 47
Kenley 32, 33
Kennedy, Air Chief Marshal Sir Thomas 129
Kent 4, 6, 12, 13
Kiddle, M. 106
kine-theodolites 36
King, C. 149
King, R. 149
King, Rt. Hon. Tom MP 152, 153
Kingdon, Obs G. P. 31
King's Lynn 8, 9
Kingsworthy post 15, 31, 86

Roome, Wing Commander D. 147
Rome (Romans) 16, 17, 64
Rommel 71
Romney Marshes 12
Rose, M. 116
Rowe, R. 140
Royal Air Force (RAF) 12, 23, 26, 31,
    33, 34, 35, 36, 41, 42, 43, 44, 45, 46,
    50, 52, 57, 58, 61, 62, 63, 64, 67, 74,
    75, 78, 80, 85, 87, 105, 109, 111,
    112, 141, 146, 147, 150, 155
Royal Artillery 7
Royal Australian Air Force 67
Royal Bath Hotel 68
Royal Canadian Air Force 67
Royal Engineers 7
Royal Flying Corps 7, 9
Royal Marines 70
Royal National Lifeboat Institution 57
Royal Navy 7, 69, 70, 118, 135
Royal New Zealand Air Force 67
Rudloe Manor 124
Ruffel-Hazel 97
Rusby, W. 105, 106
Russia 93, 124, 125
Sage, A. 60
St Albans 16
St Clement Danes 150
St Eval 33
Sands, W. 82
Sandys, D. 81
satellite posts 15, 64
Saul, Air Vice-Marshal Richard 32
Scampton 135, 139
Scott, B. 116, 140
Scott, Sir Kenneth 147
Seaborne 67, 68, 69, 70, 72, 73, 133
Seagull (Supermarine) 57
searchlights 10, 19, 20, 23, 35, 52, 63
Searle, Obs 100, 140
Selwood, K. 60
semaphore 4
Senior, G. 140
Shackleton 118
Shannon, D. 82
Shefford, A. 47

Shell Building 110
Shephard, Peter 16
Shergold, Bob 106
Sheringham 9
Shetland Islands 23, 97
Shire, C. 140
Shire, P. 140
Sholto Douglas, Air Marshal Sir W.
    63
Shrewsbury 124, 149
Shrimpton, G. 137
Shrubbs, J. 130, 148, 153
Sibley, S. 60
Sidmouth post 137
Simmonds, D. 106
Simpkins, M. 86
Simpson, Air Cdre J. 92, 97, 102
Sinclair, Sir Archibald 50
sirens 37, 38, 39, 42, 120, 121
Sismore, Air Cdre E. 110, 111, 130
Skywatch 145, 146
Slater, B. 72
Slater, K. 137
Small, W. 86
Smith, A. 140
Smith, C. 149
Smith, P. 82
Smith, J. 97, 101
Smith, R. 131
Smith T. 108
Smordon, S. 137
Snell, K. 60
Snell, N. 60
Snell, W. 60
Snow, A. 82
Snow, R. T. 15, 82, 86
snowflake/totter rockets 80
Soane, Sir John 17
sound-locators 35
South African War 7
Southampton 31, 70, 79, 81
Southeard, D. 90
Southend 33
South Wales 149
Soviet Long Range Air Force 124, 125
Soviet Union 93, 124, 125, 152, 153

174

Waterbeach 105
Watford 14, 22, 79, 88, 90, 106, 109
Watnall 32
Watson-Watt, Robert 30
Wattisham 105
Watton 135, 141
Webb, A. 82
Wedge, A. 82
Wedge, J. 75
Weeks, J. 86
Weeton 105
Wellington 90
Wembley 112
West Malling 102, 105
West Raynham 105, 135
Whitcher, M. 140
White, J. 82
Whitehall 77, 153
Whitham, J. D. 72
Whittington, J. 129
Whittle, A. 129
Wick 33
Wight-Boycott, Air Cdre C. 98, 99,
    130
Williams, S. 86
Wills, H. 106
Wills, J. 86
Wilson, R. 68
Winchester 13, 22, 56, 79, 97, 99, 101,
    103, 124, 138, 166
Windsor Castle 90
Winslow, T.E. 5
Wittering 32, 33, 47
Womens' Auxiliary Air Force
    (WAAF) 55, 64
Womens' Royal Army Corps 35
Wood, Derek 5
Wood, Sir Kingsley 23
Woodley I. 137
Worthington, F. 82
Worthington, G. 82
Worthy Down 15
Wrattan, Air Vice-Marshal Sir
    William 143
Wrexham 91, 97
Yarmouth 8, 9

Yeovil 60, 124, 127, 136, 137, 159
York 92, 98, 124, 135
zeppelins 6, 7, 8, 9, 10, 65
    L3 9
    L4 9
    L6 9
    LZ38 9